URBAN WALKS

GLASGOW
AND THE
WEST

D0470116

URBAN WALKS

GLASGOW
AND THE
WEST

ROGER SMITH

MERCAT

First published in 2009 by Mercat Press
an imprint of Birlinn Ltd
West Newington House, 10 Newington Road
Edinburgh EH9 1QS
www.birlinn.co.uk

ISBN 13: 978-1-84183-123-7

Designed and set at Birlinn

Printed and bound in Great Britain by
Bell & Bain Ltd.

CONTENTS

INTRODUCTION

The genesis for this book came in a series of articles I wrote for the Saturday magazine edition of *The Herald* newspaper every week for 2 ½ years, from October 2003 to April 2006. During this time I described over 120 urban walks in Scotland, and found it a hugely enjoyable and rewarding job.

It seemed logical to collect some of these walks together in book form and I am grateful to *The Herald* for allowing me to use some of the material which first appeared in the paper. However, all of the walks have been thoroughly revised and updated, most have been expanded to include additional material and in quite a few cases the routes have been extended and improved also.

It is worth noting that in researching the weekly urban walks, only twice did I visit a place and find insufficient material to do a walk. It reinforces my firmly held belief that all of Scotland's cities, towns and villages have a great story to tell; even the smallest and initially most unpromising of places can often come up with something quite unique. Our history in terms of architecture, townscape and people is immensely rich and varied and this I hope is reflected in the pages of this book.

This volume, which it is hoped might be the first in a series, covers Glasgow and the South-West of Scotland. The book starts with ten walks in Greater Glasgow, all of them different. Some are purely urban; some use the magnificent open spaces for which Glasgow is renowned. I could have doubled the amount of Glasgow walks without any difficulty but felt that ten was the right number for this book, so I apologise if your own favourite area is not included.

The Glasgow walks provide a good picture of how the city has developed, and indeed is continually developing today. You will visit planned suburbs such as Pollokshields and Dowanhill which have re-tained their character for over a century, and areas such as The Gorbals which have seen massive change in the past 50 years. Open spaces such as Rouken Glen, gifted by a wealthy philanthropist a century ago, Queen's Park, laid out by one of the great park designers of Victorian times, and the superb Botanic Gardens all feature.

Urban walks are necessarily short in nature, but several of the Glasgow walks can be linked together to provide longer excursions and where this is possible it is shown in the information panel.

The remaining 19 walks in the book are outwith Glasgow, stretching from Coatbridge to Helensburgh and right down to Stranraer. Several fine coastal towns such as Ayr and Largs are included as are two of my favourite places, Rothesay and Dunoon, where the short ferry ride so beloved of Glaswegians is a special feature of the outing.

An eyebrow might be raised at the inclusion of a place like Coatbridge in the book. It has however a long and fascinating history and played a crucial part in the industrial development of Central Scotland. Unlike countryside walks, urban walks do not necessarily have to be scenically attractive (though many of these are, I believe); in some cases the history is the central feature of the walk.

Being urban, the walks naturally follow roads quite a lot of the time and some of these roads are busy, so a little care is needed at crossings and junctions. Whenever possible I have tried to get off the busiest roads and use quieter routes, and in the smaller towns much of the walking is really very pleasant, and naturally relatively undemanding, meaning that these walks are very suitable for families or older people with perhaps a little less stamina than they once had. I am a coffee shop addict so have ensured there are plenty of places along the way to stop for refreshment if you feel the need!

All of the walks are accessible (very easily in most cases) by public transport. The bus and train system in the area described is excellent and I do urge you to use it. I am fortunate in that I have reached an age where bus travel is free and train fares also reduced but even if this is not the case it is much more pleasant to leave your car at home.

Architecture is naturally a major feature of these walks and the work of our most famous architects and designers is well represented. Short notes on some of them follow so that you can pick up on their work as you follow the walks. If pressed for a favourite I would probably go for William Leiper. I admire eccentrics and he combined a flair for the unusual with a strong sense of style.

I hope very much that you will enjoy following these urban walks as much as I have enjoyed putting them together. I have done my best to ensure that the information in the book (and there is a lot!) is as accurate and up-to-date as possible, but things do change, sometimes quite rapidly, so alterations will inevitably occur. I would be pleased to hear of these through the publishers for future editions.

I would like to thank Mercat Press and Birlinn for giving me the opportunity to write this book and hope it provides much pleasure and manages to tell a wee bit of Scotland's story along the way.

Roger Smith, Spring 2009

Some Major Architects

The Adam family (William, 1689-1748, Robert, 1728-92 and James, 1732-94)

Maclennan's Arch (WA, W2); Hamilton Old Parish Church (WA, W12); Obelisk, Dumfries (RA, W27); Sanquhar Tolbooth (WA, W28).

William Leiper (1839-1916)

Templeton's (W2); Dowanhill Church (the Cottier Theatre, W6); Kelvinside-Hillhead Parish Church (W6); Queen's Park Baptist Church (W8); Castlepark, Lanark (W14); The Old Academy, Dumbarton (W17).

Charles Rennie Mackintosh (1868-1926)

Glasgow School of Art and the Willow Tearooms (both W2); Southpark House (W4); The Hill House, Helensburgh (W16).

J.T.Rochead (1814-1878)

Northpark House, Ruskin Terrace, Buckingham Terrace (all W4); Levenford House (W17).

Alexander 'Greek' Thomson (1817-1875)

Eton Terrace, Lilybank House (both W4); Caledonia Road Church and his grave (both W7); Moray Place and the Double Villa (both W8); The Knowe and Nithsdale Road tenements (both W9);

Other important figures include John Baird and his son (also John), John, John James and Frank Burnet, James Miller, George Gilbert Scott, James Thomson and Charles Wilson, and you will come across their work during these walks.

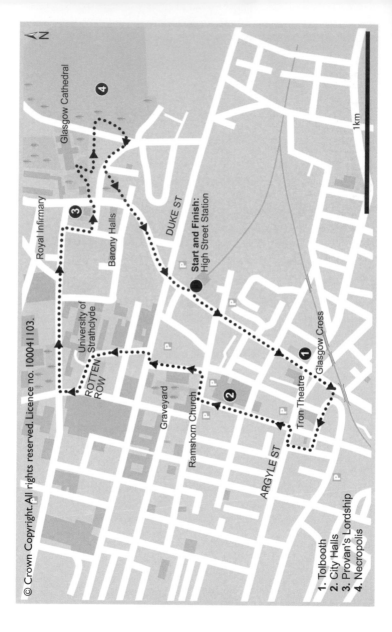

N

Royal Infirmary

Glasgow Cathedral

④

③

Barony Halls

University of Strathclyde

DUKE ST

Start and Finish: High Street Station

ROTTEN ROW

Graveyard

Ramshorn Church

②

①

Tron Theatre

Glasgow Cross

ARGYLE ST

1km

1. Tolbooth
2. City Halls
3. Provan's Lordship
4. Necropolis

THE OLD CITY

Distance	3km (2 miles) circular.
Start and Finish	High Street Station, Glasgow (or nearby car park).
Underfoot	All good paths and pavement. One short steep climb (two if you go to the top of the Necropolis).
Refreshments	Wide choice in city centre. Café at St Mungo's Museum.
Toilets	In Cathedral Square and at St Mungo's Museum (when open).
Opening hours	St Mungo's Museum and Provand's Lordship: Mon-Sat 10.00-17.00, Sun 11.00-17.00. Free. Glasgow Cathedral is open daily but please note there are services on Sunday so access may be restricted.
Further information	Free leaflets, *Glasgow's Medieval City* and *Glasgow's Medieval City: The Obscure History*, available from the Tourist Information Centre in George Square.
Links	This walk links with Walk 2 (Glasgow Green and the Barras).

This walk takes in Glasgow's oldest surviving buildings, its superb cathedral and much else. It focuses on the area covered by the original medieval city, but as relatively little of this remains, a certain amount of imagination is required.

From the station, turn left down High Street. This is where the imagination needs to kick in. Try to see it not as a modern thoroughfare busy with traffic but as the spine of the old city, connecting the cathedral with the river. These were originally two separate communities, a religious one centred round the cathedral and a secular one with trade links down by the river.

On the left was the original site of the University, founded in 1451. A 'new college' was built here in 1630, but in the mid-19th century the site became too crowded and the University moved to its present site at Gilmorehill. It is perhaps appropriate that student accommodation is still provided in the area.

Next left, where Andrew Ure Hall now stands, was the site of two priories, Blackfriars and Dominican. The latter was the older, founded in the 13th century. Both had ceased to exist by the 17th century.

Ahead is the 17th-century Tolbooth Steeple, at Glasgow Cross where four roads met and much important business was done. Try to imagine the steeple not by itself but as the endpiece of an imposing 5-storey building, the headquarters of the City Council. The jail was also here. All but the steeple was demolished in 1921. In Victorian times, this area was so overcrowded that a control system was introduced whereby metal tags were hung on doors at night to indicate the number of people sleeping inside. Public hangings were carried out at the Cross until 1814.

Tron Kirk Steeple.

A fountain here holds the old Mercat Cross and to the right you can see the Tron Kirk Steeple (1636). The kirk itself, redesigned in the 1790s by James Adam, was demolished in the 1870s.

Cross the junction into Saltmarket (a redolent name) and before the railway bridge, turn right along Parnie Street. Walk to its end and turn right on New Vennel, one of the few remaining medieval streets. You can see how narrow it is. The Vennel ran from Gallowgate down to the Briggait, by the river crossing point.

Cross Argyle Street half right into Candleriggs. Walk past Merchant Square (worth a look if you have time) and pass the beautiful 1840 City Halls, a popular venue for concerts and other events. Note by the door the plaque to the Socialist pioneer John Maclean.

Ahead is the Ramshorn Church (St David's). It provides another link with the medieval city, as the name comes from the 'Lands of Ramshorn' gifted to the Bishop of Glasgow in 1241 by King Alexander. Behind the church is a peaceful graveyard which can be explored.

Turn right and then left along Albion Street, passing the former headquarters of *The Herald* newspaper, now apartments. Cross George

Street into North Portland Street and climb steeply. Swing left on Rotten Row, noting the old archway, once part of Glasgow's main maternity hospital where untold thousands of Glasgow weans came into the world. Rotten Row is a very old street and once held fine houses and buildings belonging to the University. In its gardens is an amusing 3m high nappy pin sculpted by George Wylie.

Provand's Lordship.

Turn right along Cathedral Street past University of Strathclyde buildings. Turn right on Collins Street and (past the car park) left to reach the lovely St Nicholas Garden. This is a 'physic garden' with plants and hedges in intricate designs and also coats of arms from old buildings. The garden forms a backdrop to Provand's Lordship, Glasgow's oldest remaining dwelling. It was built in 1471 as a manse and its survival is something of a miracle. It is now a museum. Contemporary with it was St Nicholas' Hospital, of which nothing now remains.

Cross at the lights to St Mungo's Museum of Religious Life, which holds many fascinating displays. Opened in 1993, the building is in Scottish Baronial style to blend in with its surroundings, and is on the site of the old Bishop's Castle. At the rear is an intriguing Zen Garden designed by the Japanese master, Yasuatano Tanaka.

Cross the Square to the Cathedral, a powerful building that has dominated the skyline here for over 700 years. It was built on the traditional burial place of the city's patron saint, St Mungo (or Kentigern). The Lower Church is 13th-century Gothic and holds part of St Mungo's shrine.

Beyond the Cathedral is Glasgow Royal Infirmary, a rather forbidding building opened in 1914. A newer block opened in 1977.

Any church needs a graveyard, and just across from the cathedral is the extraordinary Necropolis, built on Fir Hill. The name aptly means 'city of the dead' and the place contains thousands of old memorials. To reach it, go through the elaborate gates (D. & J. Hamilton, 1838) and across the 'Bridge of Sighs'. Note on the gates the ship emblem of the

Glasgow Cathedral with a statue of David Livingstone in the foreground.

Merchants' House, which developed the cemetery from 1833 onwards. There are an estimated 50,000 graves, including a sizeable Jewish section.

You can spend hours in here. The summit holds a huge monument to John Knox and commands fine vistas of the city. This walk however turns right, downhill to the lower gate. On the left here was the Lady Well, one of the city's original sources of water. Cross Wishart Street and walk up John Knox Street.

Take the path on the left into Cathedral Square park, passing the large Peace Mosaic.

In the park is an equestrian statue to King William III – William of Orange or 'King Billy' – whose victory over the Catholic King James VII and II at the Battle of the Boyne in 1690 is still marked today by Orange Order marches.

Across the road are the Barony Halls, originally a church whose façade was modelled on Durham Cathedral. It is now used as an examination hall and for graduation ceremonies.

Walk down Castle Street (you are back on the medieval road) into High Street. The high wall on the left is all that remains of Duke Street Prison, which closed in 1955. If you look closely you may see bullet holes, from a skirmish in 1921 when an attempt was made to free Irish Republicans.

Further down High Street, on the corner of Duke Street, are fine sandstone tenements built by the City Improvement Trust in the 1870s. Their name is carved on the façade. Almost opposite the station, 215 High Street, a former bank, has a ship in stained glass above its door. This reminder of Glasgow's long maritime past neatly ends a fascinating and very varied tour.

GLASGOW GREEN AND THE BARRAS

Distance	5km (3 miles) circular.
Start and Finish	Bridgeton Station (or park near the Green).
Underfoot	All good paths and pavement.
Refreshments	Limited choice in Bridgeton area. Cafés at St Andrews in the Square, the Winter Garden and in the Barras.
Toilets	At the Winter Garden.
Opening hours	The People's Palace and Winter Gardens are open Mon-Thur and Sat 10.00-17.00, Fri and Sun 11.00-17.00. The Police Museum is open Mon-Sat 10.00-16.30, Sun 12.00-16.30 Apr-Oct, Tue 10.00-16.30, Sun 12.00-16.30 Nov-Mar. All these are free. St Andrew's in the Square is normally open on Thursday 10.30-13.00 and of course when staging concerts or other events.
Further information	Four excellent free leaflets on the Green and its history are available from the Tourist Information Centre in George Square.
Links	This walk links with the Old City (Walk 1) and also the Gorbals (Walk 7).

This walk round the area which proudly labels itself as 'Britain's oldest public space' also takes in Glasgow's renowned Barras street market. There is a huge amount to see and enjoy.

From the station, turn left, cross Dalmarnock Road and walk down Main Street for about 800 metres. Turn right on Mill Street, cross two roads and follow the path left to the car park. At the end of the car park go left down to the riverside path (also NCR75). This entry to the Green is known as Allan's Pen Gate after a 19th-century landowner who erected a 'pen' or passageway to keep people off his land. The river spirits obviously disapproved, as the Clyde rose and washed Mr Allan's pen away.

Follow the path along beside the Clyde, a very pleasant walk. Above you is the eastern area of Glasgow Green, known as Flesher's Haugh. Fleshers were butchers and there were once abattoirs here, but for the past century the area has been used for recreation.

Pass under Polmadie Bridge. Across the river is Richmond Park,

WALK 2

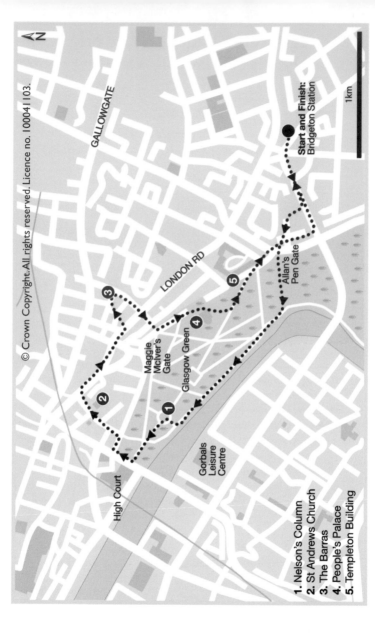

N

GALLOWGATE

LONDON RD

High Court

Maggie McIver's Gate

Glasgow Green

Allan's Pen Gate

Gorbals Leisure Centre

Start and Finish: Bridgeton Station

1km

1. Nelson's Column
2. St Andrews Church
3. The Barras
4. People's Palace
5. Templeton Building

recently renovated, and the new Richmond Gate/Oatlands development, almost a new village and yet another phase in Glasgow's continual process of renewal. The name comes from Sir David Richmond, Lord Provost at the time the park was created in 1900.

The river makes a big swing right (north) to King's Bridge. Across the river here is the Gorbals (Walk 7). Pass under the bridge and go up the steps on the right to take the upper path. This is Bonnie Prince Charlie's Gate. In December 1745, the Prince's troops assembled here, threatening to besiege the city. There is a good view downriver.

At a fork go left. Pass St Andrew's Suspension Bridge and the lifeboat house. The bridge was opened in 1854 to enable

The Nelson Monument.

workers to reach factories on the south side more easily.

Now follow the broad path to Nelson's Monument with the Winter Gardens to the right. Over 40m high, David Hamilton's obelisk was completed in 1806, a year after the Battle of Trafalgar, and predates the better-known column in London.

From the monument follow the main avenue to MacLennan's Arch, passing a fountain dedicated to Sir William Collins, Lord Provost of Glasgow from 1877-1880 and a noted campaigner for temperance. The massive arch was presented to the city by Bailie James MacLennan in 1843 (some gift!), and believe it or not was originally at first floor level on the 1792 Adam-designed Assembly Rooms in Ingram Street. The arch has been bodily moved three times, so let us hope it is now at rest!

Beyond the arch is an area known as Jocelyn Square, the scene of 71 public executions in the 19th century. Among those hanged here was James 'Pearly' Wilson, who we also meet in Strathaven (Walk 11). The last hanging, in 1865, was of Dr Edward Pritchard, who poisoned his wife and mother. He was hanged during the Glasgow Fair in front of a huge crowd estimated at 80,000.

WALK 2

Turn right. Across the road is the grand 1814 High Court by William Stark. Turn right on Greendyke Street past Mumford's Gate, where one of Glasgow's popular 'penny geggie' theatres ran until the 1870s. Take the first left at St Andrew's-by-the-Green, a lovely 1750 former church now housing the Glasgow Association for Mental Health. Walk past the District Court to the superb St Andrew's in the Square. Built 1754, the church, to a design by Dreghorn and Naismith based on St Martin's in the Fields in London, has recently been fully restored and is now a cultural centre for Scottish music and dance.

The Doulton Fountain.

Opposite the church is Glasgow Police Museum, less well known than some of Glasgow's other museums but very much worth a visit.

Continue to London Road and turn right. At the lights fork left and continue to The Barras, Glasgow's famous 'flea market'. The maze of small alleys is best seen at weekends when all the stalls are occupied and you can buy almost anything here at bargain prices. Explore the area at your leisure. When you are ready to leave, exit to Bain Street and turn right. Cross London Road and walk back down to the Green at Maggie McIver's Gate, named for the founder of The Barras and the Barrowland Ballroom. Maggie died in 1958 aged 79.

Turn left along the roadway to the astonishing Doulton Fountain, the largest and finest terracotta fountain in the world. Designed by A.E. Pearce, it was built for an international exhibition at Kelvingrove Park in 1888, moved to the Green two years later and to its present site in 2004, when it was fully restored and reopened. Queen Victoria sits atop it, and carvings represent her Empire. When floodlit at night it is quite magnificent.

Cross to the People's Palace and Winter Garden. Opened in 1898, the Palace is a superb museum of local history and culture. The beautiful glass Winter Gardens have staged many concerts, shows and exhibitions in the past. There are fine plants inside and a café if you need a break.

People's Palace and Winter Garden.

Leave by the back gate and turn left past the small fountain dedicated to Hugh MacDonald, the 19th-century journalist whose books of walks around the city are classics still read today. The fountain was originally on Gleniffer Braes near Paisley.

Reach the road and walk along the edge of the Green, with Templeton's to the left. This extraordinary 1889 William Leiper building with its multi-coloured brick gives full expression to the often eccentric ideas that Leiper came up with. It was modelled on the Doge's Palace in Venice. Originally a carpet factory, the building was the scene of a tragedy shortly after it opened when part collapsed, killing 29 female workers.

It is now a business centre, one of the occupants being a microbrewery. Beyond it is the ornate Martin Fountain (1893), then, at 47 Greenhead Street, the former Buchanan Institute for Destitute Children (1846, Charles Wilson). Note the touching carving of a boy studying his slate.

Cross the road at the lights and walk back up James Street to the station. Hugh MacDonald wrote in 1854 that 'few towns can boast such a spacious and beautiful park as the Green of Glasgow'. His words ring true today, a tribute both to James Cleland, the Superintendent of Public Works who oversaw the laying out of the Green in 1815-1826, and to today's City Council who with numerous partners have worked imaginatively and effectively to restore and enhance the Green.

It actually holds more trees and shrubs now than at any time in its history and is, as I am sure you will agree, a true pleasure to visit at any time of the year.

WALK 2

9

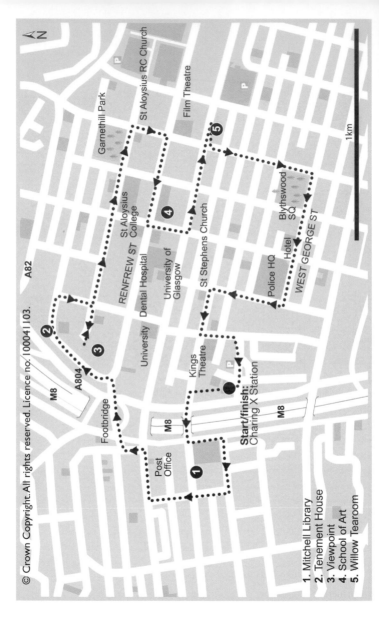

N

A82

M8

A804

Footbridge

University

RENFREW ST

St Aloysius College

Garnethill Park

St Aloysius RC Church

Dental Hospital

University of Glasgow

St Stephens Church

Film Theatre

Kings Theatre

Post Office

M8

M8

Police HQ

Hotel

Blythswood SQ

WEST GEORGE ST

Start/finish:
Charing X Station

1km

1. Mitchell Library
2. Tenement House
3. Viewpoint
4. School of Art
5. Willow Tearoom

BLYTHSWOOD AND GARNETHILL

Distance	3km (2 miles) circular.
Start and Finish	Charing Cross Station, Glasgow.
Underfoot	All good paths and pavement. Two short steep climbs.
Public transport	Regular trains and buses from the city centre.
Refreshments	Wide choice in city centre. Café at the Mitchell Library.
Toilets	Mitchell Library (when open).
Opening hours	The Tenement House is open daily, 13.00-17.00, from 1 March to 31 October. For tours phone 0844 493 2197. Tours of the School of Art are available – phone 0141 353 4526 for details.

Great architecture, a Victorian scandal and a surprising view are among the features of this intriguing walk. Leaving the station, turn right up steps under an office block, go down to the road and turn left. There is a beautiful old tree here which holds a brave show of white blossom in spring. Cross the motorway and turn left on North Street to walk round the Mitchell Library. This magnificent building, which has recently undergone extensive refurbishment, holds the largest public reference library in Europe.

The original entrance (1911, William Whitie) is in North Street. Pass it, turn right and right again into Granville Street to see the library's imposing frontage with 16 statues by John Mossman representing literature, painting, architecture and music. This was originally the façade of the St Andrew's Halls. Emily Pankhurst held a major suffragette meeting here in 1914, during which a riot broke out.

Seriously damaged by fire in 1962, the building was rebuilt and extended between 1972 and 1980. Over the main entrance are two Atlanteans by William Mossman. The library has a wide range of facilities, a café and toilets.

Cross Sauchiehall Street and turn right. At the Cameron Memorial Fountain (named for a 19th-century MP) go left, then right to re-cross the motorway on a footbridge. At the far side, look ahead along Renfrew Street – can you see the large bust of Beethoven on no 341 (formerly the rear of a music shop)?

Mitchell Library entrance, Granville Street.

Turn left and walk along Buccleuch Street, which initially has no pavement, so care is needed. Reach no 145, the Tenement House. Owned by the National Trust for Scotland, it was bequeathed by Miss Agnes Toward, who had not altered the apartment in over 50 years, and is a fascinating 'time capsule'. Turn right up Garnet Street (a steep climb) and right again to the end of Hill Street for a surprising viewpoint. The wide panorama takes in the West End, the University and extends out to the Kilpatrick Hills.

Walk back along Hill Street. On the right is the Garnethill Synagogue (1879, John McLeod), the first of its kind in Scotland and still in regular use today. Continue across Scott Street. On the right is St Aloysius College (1882, Archibald MacPherson, in the style of a Venetian palazzo). Next left is Garnethill Park, a joint Scottish-German project opened in 1991. The large mural (sadly defaced by graffiti) is made from over 180,000 pieces of tile. Turn right into Rose Street to see St Aloysius RC Church. This is a gem, a 1908 design by Charles Menart in an Italianate style which is continued inside – the interior is sumptuous, with much marble and mosaic.

Turn right into Renfrew Street and continue to the Glasgow School of Art. Whole books have been written about Mackintosh's masterpiece. Built between 1897 and 1909, the building contains much superb detail and is a veritable shrine for devotees of CRM. It has a Mackintosh Museum, and guided tours can be arranged. It is still very much a working building.

Turn left into Scott Street – this is very steep downhill, so take care. Turn left on Sauchiehall Street and continue to the McLellan Galleries. Built for a Victorian collector, the building briefly housed the School of Art and was for a time a department store, before reverting to its original function.

Just past Blythswood Street are the Willow Tea Rooms, converted by Mackintosh for Kate Cranston in 1903. Much of the interior is original and is unmistakeably Mackintosh in its design. The name is taken from the Gaelic meaning of Sauchiehall, 'place of willows'. Kate Cranston was a notable patron to artists and architects. It was her brother who first had the idea of providing tea and cakes for people at a modest charge. Kate's first premises were in Argyle Street in 1878 and she opened others at regular intervals.

Return to Blythswood Street and turn left up to Blythswood Square. On the corner at nos 6-7 is Madeleine Smith House. In 1857 Madeleine (who lived here) was accused of murdering her lover Pierre l'Angelier with arsenic. The case became so notorious in Glasgow that the trial was held in Edinburgh where the jury, unconvinced by the prosecution's evidence, returned a verdict of 'Not Proven'. We meet Madeleine again on Walk 10.

Continue past the former Royal Scottish Automobile Club building, which takes up the whole east side of the square, and turn right along West George Street. Pass the Malmaison Hotel, formerly St Jude's Church. The Greek inscription means 'God is head of the church'. Cross Pitt Street (noting the HQ of Strathclyde Police on the right), turn right into Holland Street, and walk up to Bath Street. Turn left. Across the road is Renfield St Stephens Church, designed by John T. Emmett and opened in 1852.

Turn left at the King's Theatre into Elmbank Street. The King's is a fantasy in red sandstone, designed by Frank Matcham and opened in 1904. It remains one of Glasgow's most popular venues for musicals, pantomimes and other shows. Inside there is a fine picture gallery. Turn right along Elmbank Crescent back to the station.

WALK 3

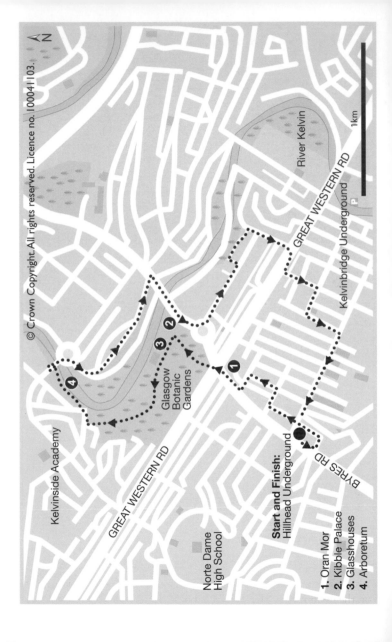

N

River Kelvin

GREAT WESTERN RD

Kelvinbridge Underground

Kelvinside Academy

GREAT WESTERN RD

Glasgow Botanic Gardens

Norte Dame High School

BYRES RD

Start and Finish: Hillhead Underground

1. Oran Mor
2. Kibble Palace
3. Glasshouses
4. Arboretum

1km

HILLHEAD AND THE BOTANIC GARDENS

Distance	3km (2 miles) circular.
Start and Finish	Hillhead Underground Station.
Underfoot	All good paths and pavement.
Public transport	Regular subway service from Glasgow city centre.
Refreshments	Wide choice in Byres Road area. Kiosk cafe at the Botanic Gardens.
Toilets	In the Botanic Gardens.
Opening hours	The Botanic Gardens are open daily, 9am-sunset. The Kibble Palace and glasshouses are open 10.00-18.00 in summer and 10.00-16.15 in winter, and the visitor centre is open 11.00-16.00 daily. Admission is free.
Links	This walk can easily be linked with Walk 5, Kelvingrove and the University and Walk 6, Dowanhill.

This walk explores a fascinating part of Glasgow's West End and also the city's magnificent Botanic Gardens. From the station, turn left and left again into Ashton Lane, passing one of Glasgow's best-known restaurants, the Ubiquitous Chip. Turn left into the cobbled Great George Lane. Cross Great George Street into Cresswell Lane, past De Courcy's Arcade with its interesting small shops.

Turn right on Cresswell Street and left on Cranworth Street, passing the Western Baths Club (1876) with its grand Gothic entrance. Turn left on Vinicombe Street. The domed building on the left is the former Salon Cinema (1912), a classic of its period. It closed to filmgoers in 1992 and is now a restaurant and bar. The former Botanics Garage (also 1912) has lovely old green and white tiling known as 'faience'.

Turn right on Byres Road to reach Oran Mor, an arts and music centre housed in the former Kelvinside Parish Church (designed by J.J.Stevenson in 1862). The centre hosts a busy programme of events and has restaurants and a bar. Its graceful spire is a notable local landmark.

Cross the main roads diagonally (and carefully) to enter the Botanic Gardens. Note the city coat of arms on the lodge house. Keep on the main path to the famous Kibble Palace, a superb glass building built for John Kibble in 1865, brought here from his Coulport home in 1873, and recently fully restored in a large-scale project which had Heritage Lottery funding. For a few years, the Palace was used as a venue for concerts and meetings, but since 1881 has held plants. It now contains a number of fine white marble statues including *Eve* and *Cain*, and houses the National Tree-Fern Collection – and a section devoted to 'killer plants', which are happily dangerous only to insects, not humans!

Believe it or not, you are above a former railway line here, and can actually see down into the site of the Botanics Station, opened in 1896 but in use only until 1939.

There is a lot to see in the Gardens, and hours can easily slip away here. Follow the signs to the main range of glasshouses, which hold a wondrous array of exotic plants and also the National Collection of Begonias. There are tropical ferns, rare orchids, even bananas growing.

On leaving the far end of the glasshouses, follow the main path up a little way, then go left to walk through the herb and scented gardens. Continue past the Scottish Bed (which includes tormentil, hart's tongue fern and wormwood) and the vegetable beds, to the Chronological Garden, with plants arranged in the order they were introduced to Britain. The 16th-century section includes carnations, peonies and rue. On the right is the World Rose Garden and, near the flagpole, a memorial stone to the much-loved entertainer, Jimmy Logan.

The Kibble Palace in the Botanic Gardens.

Continue on the main path, curving left to leave the Gardens at the Kirklee Gate.

Turn sharp right (Ford Road), downhill to the River Kelvin. On the right is the Ha'penny Bridge, the latest in a series which have stood here for over 200 years. When first opened it carried a toll of a halfpenny, hence its name. Go through the gate into the Arboretum, laid out from 1900 onwards and holding many splendid trees. Go under the beautiful Kirklee Bridge, opened in 1901 and with superb polished granite pillars. At the far side, go left up steps, then left again at the road to cross the bridge.

Turn right on Kelvin Drive. On the left, Botanic Crescent makes a grand sweep of houses overlooking

The River Kelvin.

the river. Cross the road and turn right over Queen Margaret Bridge. On the left is Northpark House (J.T.Rochead, 1869), a large Italianate mansion with fine Doric columns. Turn left on Hamilton Drive. On the right here is Northpark Terrace, a rather plain design of 1868 by 'Greek' Thomson.

Continue past the former Scottish headquarters of the BBC. The Corporation moved here in 1935, and countless well-known radio and TV programmes were produced in this complex. The BBC moved in summer 2007 to a new complex on the south side of the Clyde.

Turn left on Hamilton Park and follow the road right, with the river below to the left. A little way along, go right on a path through an attractive small garden and then right again on an odd little cobbled lane that winds between the houses. Go left and right with the lane to reach Great Western Road. On the right is Ruskin Terrace (1855) followed by Buckingham Terrace (1852), reflecting the importance of the thoroughfare in Victorian times. Both were designed by Rochead and have fine detailing including some cast iron balconies.

WALK 4

Eton Terrace.

Cross the road into Oakfield Avenue. Just past Glasgow Street, on the left, is a block of 8 houses originally known as Eton Terrace; they are a typical 'Greek' Thomson design. Turn right on Gibson Sreet. On the far side of Southpark Avenue is Southpark House (1850), the last villa to be built in Hillhead. Charles Rennie Mackintosh lived in this area from 1906 to 1914. His home's interiors have been recreated as the Mackintosh House in the Hunterian Art Gallery.

Turn left on Hillhead Street. On the corner is Florentine House, one of the oldest houses in the area (1828). Take the first path on the right, through the University buildings, and reach a courtyard in front of Lilybank House, with its fine portico. When built in the 1830s it stood in 12 acres of ornamental gardens. It was remodelled in the 1860s by 'Greek' Thomson, and later further refurbished by Honeyman & Keppie, for whom Mackintosh worked. It is believed to be the only house worked on by both these great architects.

Turn right through a gate onto a road, then left on Great George Street to return to the start – or perhaps to enjoy a coffee or a drink in one of the many cosmopolitan bars and eating places around Byres Road. On the way you pass the former Belmont Parish Church (1892), one of James Miller's first successful designs.

KELVINGROVE AND THE UNIVERSITY

Distance	4km (2.5 miles) circular.
Start and Finish	Kelvin Bridge subway station.
Underfoot	All good paths and pavement.
Public transport	Frequent subway trains and buses to Kelvin Bridge from the city centre.
Refreshments	Good choice in Kelvin Bridge area. Cafés at the University Visitor Centre and Kelvingrove Museum.
Toilets	At the University Visitor Centre, the Museum and in the park.
Opening hours	University Visitor Centre: Mon-Sat 09.30-17.00, Sun (summer only) 14.00-17.00. Hunterian Museum: Mon-Sat 09.30-17.00. Free. Hunterian Art Gallery and the Mackintosh House: Mon-Sat 10.00-17.00. Museum free, admission charge for the Mackintosh House. Kelvingrove Art Gallery and Museum: Mon-Thur, Sat 10.00-17.00; Fri, Sun 11.00-17.00. Free. Websites: www.glasgow.ac.uk and www.glasgowmuseums.com.
Links	This walk links with Walk 4 (Hillhead and the Botanic Gardens).

This varied and attractive walk explores the open spaces of Glasgow's popular Kelvingrove Park, tours part of the University and includes several superb museums.

From Kelvin Bridge, walk down the steps beside the subway station, cross the car park and continue on a path through a small park. Go up steps to the bridge and turn right across the River Kelvin. Follow Gibson Street to the lights, turn left and curve right, uphill, on University Avenue into the Glasgow University complex. Turn left through the ornamental gates (gifted in 1951) to the area containing the Visitor Centre, where you can get a map. Inside the gates is a memorial to William and John Hunter, the brothers who bequeathed their collections to the university.

Glasgow University was established in 1471 down in the old part of the city (see Walk 1) but, needing more space, moved to this area on Gilmorehill in 1870. The main building was designed by Sir Giles Gilbert Scott, and the tower, which was completed by his son John Oldrid Scott in 1888, is over 100m high. The guided tours of the University sometimes take you to the top of the tower, an exciting climb up a very

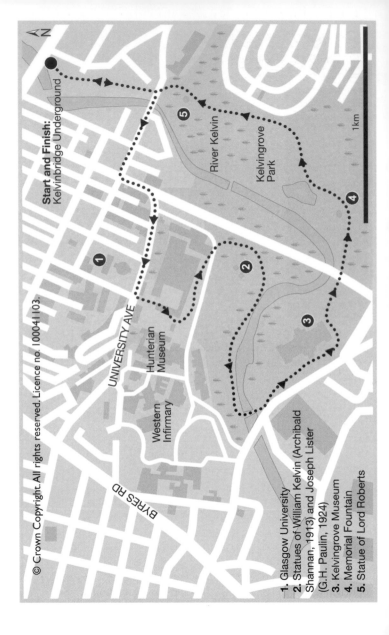

Start and Finish:
Kelvinbridge Underground

1 km

UNIVERSITY AVE

BYRES RD

Western Infirmary

Hunterian Museum

River Kelvin

Kelvingrove Park

N

1. Glasgow University
2. Statues of William Kelvin (Archibald Shannan, 1913) and Joseph Lister (G.H. Paulin, 1924)
3. Kelvingrove Museum
4. Memorial Fountain
5. Statue of Lord Roberts

Glasgow University.

narrow spiral staircase – definitely not for claustrophobics! The views from the top are superb in all directions.

Leave the Visitor Centre and go up the stone staircase, which brings you out into the East Quadrangle – a typical university space with the open area flanked by the original 1870 buildings. On the right is the Hunterian Museum, Scotland's oldest public museum (opened in 1807, just 200 years ago) and holding over a million items. The Hunterian reopened in May 2007 after extensive refurbishment.

Turn right through the arches to the West Quadrangle. Facing you is the university chapel, opened in 1929 and dedicated to those who lost their lives in the 1914-18 War. It can be accessed by going through the Chaplaincy building. Outside the chapel is the Lion and Unicorn Staircase, part of the original university and reassembled here – with the stair turning the opposite way!

Leaving the chapel, turn left to the South Front which affords good views over the city. Go left along the South Front past the James Watt Building with its impressive mural and then down steps to the right, to reach Kelvin Way. Turn right. Across the road are toilets and also the old bandstand and auditorium, currently awaiting restoration. Take the first path on the right, leading back down towards the river. You pass statues of Kelvin (Archibald Shannan, 1913) and Lister (G.H.Paulin, 1924).

WALK 5

William Kelvin (1824-1907) was an astonishing man. He was admitted to Glasgow University at the age of 10 and was a professor at 22. He was a profuse inventor. His house in Glasgow was the first to be lit by electricity; he was chief consultant for the laying of the first Atlantic cable in 1857; and he developed the scale of absolute temperature which still carries his name.

Joseph Lister (1827-1912) was not a Scot but did most of his best work here, including the development of antiseptics, which revolutionised surgery. He often walked in the Park before breakfast.

Behind the statues is the Pulham Rockery and Cascade, erected for the 1901 Exhibition and one of only three Pulham rockeries in Scotland. The cascade does not function at present but may be restored in the future.

Statue of Lister in Kelvingrove Park.

Follow the path down to the river, passing Benno Schotz's semi-abstract sculpture called *The Psalmist*. Continue beside the river – a very attractive walk – noting on the left the Bunhouse Weir, once part of the old Bishop's Mills of Partick. Walk up to the road, and turn left over the bridge. This is the older Partick Bridge (1800), no longer used for traffic. It was called the Snowbridge, as gates on its south-west side were used to allow snow to be swept into the river in winter.

On the right is Kelvin Hall and the Museum of Transport. On the left is the A-listed Kelvingrove Museum and Art Gallery. Designed in 1901 by Simpson and Allan in Spanish Baroque style, it is built of warm Dumfriesshire sandstone. It has recently undergone extensive refurbishment. The museum, one of the finest in Britain, has an astonishing range of displays, far too many to mention here. You can spend hours in here. It also has a superb organ and the regular recitals are well worth attending.

Leave the museum, turn left and left again round the outside of the building. Turn right at the car park, past George Wylie's amusing sculpture of the *Vital Spark*, the 'puffer' skippered by Para Handy in Neil Munro's timeless stories. Cross the road into Kelvingrove Park. The park was originally laid out by Sir Joseph Paxton in 1852 and is very typical of its period, spacious and open, with many fine trees. It is regarded as one of the first fully designed parks in Scotland.

Curve left with the main path and then go right across a garden to see the memorial fountain to Robert Stewart, Lord Provost of Glasgow, who was instrumental in setting up the scheme which provided piped water from Loch Katrine in the Trossachs to supply Glasgow's ever-expanding needs in the 1860s. The statues are based on themes from Walter Scott's *Lady of the Lake*, which is set around Loch Katrine.

From the fountain, walk down to the pond and turn right. The island in the pond is shaped like Cyprus, though this is not immediately obvious! At the next junction turn right, then fork left twice.

River Kelvin and the University.

At a statue of a tigress with a peacock (by Auguste Cain), presented to his native city in 1867 by John S. Kennedy of New York, go left, uphill, cross a path, then turn left on the main path. There is an excellent view of the University buildings. This part of the park has fine birch and beech trees.

Keep on the main path to the large equestrian statue of Lord Roberts, VC (an exact replica of a statue in Calcutta, India – Roberts won his VC during the Indian Mutiny). It quotes part of a speech he made in May 1913, in which he talks of "the pledge of the peace and of the continued greatness of the Empire". Within a year the world would be plunged into the unimaginable horror of the Great War. Roberts himself died, aged 82, while visiting troops in France in November 1914.

From the statue go left, downhill, and follow the paths out to the road. The large building to the right is part of Glasgow Caledonian University. Cross the road, with St Silas Episcopal Church to your right, and go back down the steps to the station.

WALK 5

23

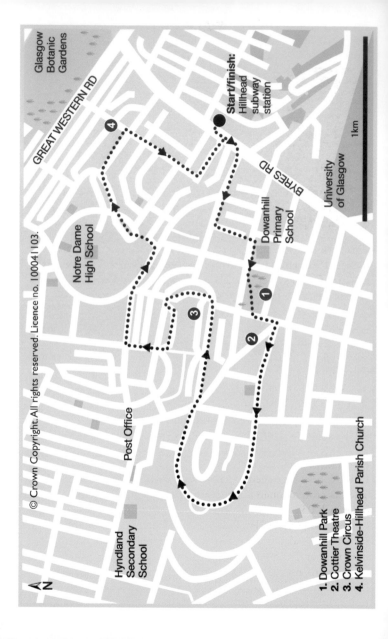

Glasgow Botanic Gardens

GREAT WESTERN RD

Start/finish: Hillhead subway station

BYRES RD

University of Glasgow

1 km

Notre Dame High School

Dowanhill Primary School

Post Office

Hyndland Secondary School

1. Dowanhill Park
2. Cottier Theatre
3. Crown Circus
4. Kelvinside-Hillhead Parish Church

N

DOWANHILL

Distance	3km (2 miles) circular.
Start and Finish	Hillhead subway station.
Underfoot	All good paths and pavement.
Public transport	Frequent subway trains and buses to Hillhead from the city centre.
Refreshments	Good choice in Hillhead area.
Toilets	None on the route.
Further information	A set of excellent free leaflets covering Dowanhill, Hyndland & Partickhill, Hillhead, Kelvinside and Partick is available locally.
Links	This walk links with Walk 4 (Hillhead and the Botanic Gardens).

This walk enables us to follow the westward expansion of Glasgow in the mid-19th century as the city prospered and grew. Landowners (in this case Thomas Paterson) developed suburban estates on the western edge of the city for people seeking spacious accommodation, in conjunction with the new turnpike roads that were being built. Dowanhill is a good example of this development.

From Hillhead Station, cross Byres Road, turn left and then right on Dowanhill Road. This junction has long been known as Victoria Cross. On the right you soon see the first of many graceful arcs of housing, Victoria Crescent, designed by the prolific James Thomson. Turn left on Caledon Street past Dowanhill Tennis Club and then right on Highburgh Road. On the corner is the Western Exchange, built as a telephone exchange in 1907 with accommodation also provided.

Pass Dowanhill Primary School (1894, typical of its era in its rather forbidding design) and cross Dowanhill Street to enter the small Dowanhill Park, opened in 1904 and known locally as the Wee Park. The cast iron fountain adorned with herons was restored to working order in 2003.

Exit the park on Havelock Street and cross Hyndland Street into Partickhill Road, passing the former Dowanhill Church, now the well-used Cottier Theatre complex. William Leiper's superb 1865 design (at the age of just 26) is in Normandy Gothic with a glorious spire. The interior features magnificent decoration by Daniel Cottier, still being restored through the efforts of a trust fund.

WALK 6

25

Victoria Crescent, Dowanhill.

Continue past Partickhill Bowling and Tennis Club, established a century ago. On the right are two significant houses. No 56, Woodbank, is a beautiful small villa built about 1840 with a Greek Ionic porch. Over the past 160 years the house has, amazingly, only had three owners. At no 64 is 'Mr Robb's House', the oldest building in the West End. Dating from 1794, it was built for James Robb, lawyer and landowner. He later sold the land to William Hamilton, who began the development of the surrounding streets.

Continue round the curve into Turnberry Road. Redclyffe, on the left, was the first house in the West End to be built of red sandstone (1871). Reach Hyndland Road and cross (with care) into Crown Road South. On the left, behind the trees, is James Thomson's impressive Crown Terrace.

You then reach Crown Circus, the showpiece of the estate. This too is by Thomson, a very strong curve dating from 1858 which has been a desirable address ever since. Many of the houses have recently had their stonework cleaned. On the right you pass a double villa, Royston and Wendel. The former was the home of Dr Archibald Barr, founder of the optical instrument company Barr & Stroud. Wendel was worked on internally by Charles Rennie Mackintosh.

Turn left into Victoria Circus, which features a number of elegant detached villas, of which Elstow (no 5) is perhaps the best. On the left you see Kensington Tower, an Italianate villa of 1858 with a campanile. Close to it is Northcote, now used as a surgery. Continue around Kensington Gate, a particularly interesting curved terrace designed by David Barclay and featuring decorative glass and polished red granite columns.

Turn left onto Dundonald Road at St Luke's Cathedral, designed by James Sellars and opened as a Presbyterian church on this prominent site in 1877. The front features superb tall lancet windows and the interior has lovely stained glass by Stephen Adam. The building is now used as a cathedral by the area's Greek Orthodox community.

Continue along Dundonald Road, which is at the boundary of the original Dowanhill Estate, leading into the area known as Victoria Park. The houses here were completed between 1870 and 1900.

Pass the entrance to Notre Dame High School and curve left past Marleybank, built 1840 for a Glasgow lawyer called Robert Sword. It has a fine Doric portico with fluted columns. The stained glass window is thought to be by Cottier. Turn sharp right on Huntly Gardens and walk down to Saltoun Street. Turn right.

On the left is Kelvinside-Hillhead Parish Church, a powerful Gothic design of 1876. There was a competition to decide the design: although this was won by James Sellars, he was apparently asked to largely use the design of the runner-up, William Leiper! Whoever was responsible, the result (which was inspired by Sainte-Chappelle in Paris) is magnificent, with soaring towers and buttresses.

Kelvinside-Hillhead Parish Church.

Continue along Saltoun Street, passing Athole Gardens on the left. Note the building at the corner of Ruthven Street, an intriguing L-shaped tenement with rounded ends. Unusually, it has a double in Novar Drive in Hyndland. Both date from around 1905.

Turn left down Ruthven Lane, one of a number of fascinating narrow lanes in this area. Crammed with interesting small shops, cafes and restaurants, they are a delight to explore. Many of the buildings were originally garages or stables. A gentle wander down the lane will lead you back to Byres Road almost opposite the subway station.

WALK 6

27

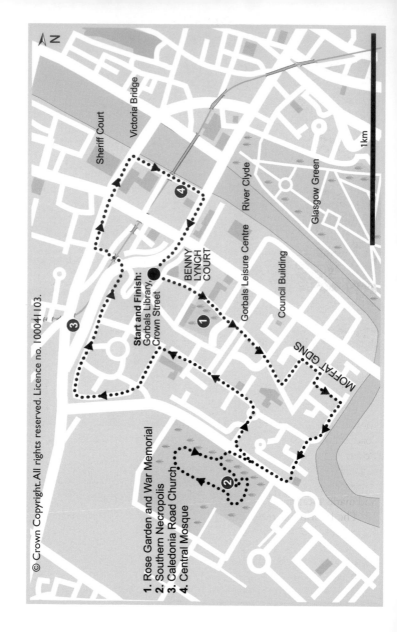

1. Rose Garden and War Memorial
2. Southern Necropolis
3. Caledonia Road Church
4. Central Mosque

Start and Finish:
Gorbals Library,
Crown Street

BENNY LYNCH COURT

Gorbals Leisure Centre

Council Building

MOFFAT GDNS

River Clyde

Glasgow Green

Sheriff Court

Victoria Bridge

N

1km

THE GORBALS

Distance	3km (2 miles) circular.
Start and Finish	Gorbals Library, Crown Street.
Underfoot and access	Pavement and good paths. The walk is wheelchair-accessible (short flight of steps into the Rose Garden).
Public transport	Short bus journey from Glasgow city centre or an easy walk from Central Station.
Refreshments	Limited choice in the area (tearoom and café/deli in Crown Street), but the city centre is not far away.
Toilets	None on the route.
Opening hours	The Central Mosque has a museum, open daily except Thurs and Fri, 10.00-12.00, free. You can sometimes see the prayer area but must arrange this in advance through 0141 429 3132.
Further information	Visit www.theartworksprogramme.org and www.gorbalsartsproject.org. The Gorbals Historical Guide and Heritage Walk by Ronald Smith is available from Gorbals Library, price £6.99. A very good Southern Necropolis Heritage Trail booklet is available free, either locally or from the Tourist Information Centre in George Square.
Links	This walk can be linked with Walk 2 (Glasgow Green and the Barras).

The Gorbals area has seen almost continual redevelopment since the 1950s and is still a 'work in progress'. As this walk shows, the latest changes include excellent public art.

From the library, turn left (Crown Street) and right into Old Rutherglen Road, noting the unusual metal wall mounting of the Glasgow coat of arms. Pass Benny Lynch Court, named for a famous Glasgow boxer. Cross Pine Place and turn right into the Rose Garden, a former cemetery. Its central feature is a beautiful war memorial in the form of a rose, sculpted by Liz Peden. The base is shaped like a Victoria Cross and marks local man James Stokes, awarded the VC in 1945.

The inscription reads 'stop and look, really look, tomorrow may be too late'. East of the Memorial are two further artworks: Amanda Currie's Public Orchard and Cultivated Wilderness by Matt Baker and Sans Facon.

Return to Old Rutherglen Road and turn right. Pass Spring Wynd and Queen Elizabeth Gardens, a recent attractive redevelopment. Note

WALK 7

The Gatekeeper sculpture by Matt Baker and Dan Dubowitz.

David Ralston's metal *Bird Catcher* sculptures over the doorways of the latter.

Cross Waddell Street and pass the Hayfield Centre for deaf people. Turn left on Moffat Street and right, through Moffat Gardens, to see the 6m pavement mosaic in black and white featuring a magpie, heron and swans. Note also the amusing 'pine cone' bollards.

Go right and left into Turnlaw Street and right on Waterside Street, beside the Clyde. Across the river is Glasgow Green (Walk 2). Follow the road right and left into Silverfir Street. Walk up to Caledonia Road, cross and turn right, along to the imposing gateway to the Southern Necropolis, erected in 1848. The Necropolis holds over

250,000 graves, mainly from Victorian times. Behind it is the area still known as Dixon's Blazes, after the fires from blast furnaces when there was an iron works here. The area is named for the industrialist John Dixon, who developed it.

Turn left through the gateway. The Necropolis contains many interesting memorials but there is only room to mention a few here. The booklet listed in the information panel describes many more.

Inside the gate, turn left on the path and look for the small marker no 1 on the left. It refers to the large cartouche on the wall commemorating Dr Nathaniel Paterson, one of the leaders of the breakaway movement which formed the Free Church in the 1840s. Continue round the bend to find no 2, the obelisk to Peter Ferguson, founder of the Band of

Pavement mosaic in Moffat Gardens.

Hope movement and a leading campaigner for temperance.

Go through the gateway in the wall, turn left and follow the path down and round to the right. In the far corner is a memorial to Agnes Harkness (no 7), called the Heroine of Matagorda for her bravery during a battle in Spain in 1810. A little further up on the right is the rather modest monument to Sir Thomas Lipton. Sir Thomas, who founded a chain of grocery stores and a famous tea company, was born in Crown Street in 1850. From humble beginnings, he became a millionaire. A noted sailor, he contested the America's Cup (unsuccessfully) five times.

Turn right on the next path, go back through the gateway and turn left. Look for an arrow leading you right, across the grass to no 14 (by the bushes). It commemorates Charles Wilson, a noted architect who designed the Necropolis gatehouse and was involved with the plans for Park Circus in Glasgow's West End among many other fine buildings.

Continue across the Central Path and straight ahead on the grass to no 21, the White Lady, one of the Necropolis's most famous monuments. It marks the resting place of Magdalene Smith and her

WALK 7

31

housekeeper Mary McNaughton, who tragically died while returning from church on 29 October 1933. Sheltering from heavy rain beneath an umbrella, they failed to see an approaching tramcar, which struck and killed them. It is said that the White Lady turns her head as you pass by.

Caledonia Road Church.

Walk across to the gateway in the wall and follow the path ahead to the distinctive memorial to the great architect 'Greek' Thomson (no 26). It simply bears the word 'Thomson' and is a striking design in black marble erected here in 2006. Walk back through the gateway and continue to the central rotunda, the burial place of Franciscan monks, reinterred here in 2005. Walk down the Central Pathway to the gatehouse.

Leave the Necropolis, cross the road, turn left and then first right into Cumberland Street, continuing along and left to reach the beautiful St Francis Centre, a former Friary. The building, designed by Gilbert Blount, dates from 1870. It fell derelict, but a partnership including Glasgow Building Preservation Trust and the National Trust for Scotland restored it and, reopened in 1997, it enjoys a new life as a community centre and amenity flats for the elderly.

Outside Queen Elizabeth Gardens is *Gorbals Boys*, Liz Peden's superb sculptural realisation of the famous Marzaroli photo of three urchins wearing their mothers' high heels. Just past the police station is Kenny Hunter's sculpture of *Girl with a Rucksack*. Turn left into Camden Terrace, cross to Kidston Place and turn right along Kidston Terrace, noting the striking *Attendants* over the doorways. Continue to the corner to look up at the impressive *Gatekeeper* suspended high above. Both these works were created by Heisenberg: Matt Baker and Dan Dubowitz.

Turn right down Malta Terrace. Across the road is 'Greek' Thomson's Caledonia Road Church, now a stark ruin but once one of his most impressive works. Built in 1857, it has a majestic Ionic portico. The church was severely damaged by fire in 1965 but is still A-listed.

This area was known as Hutchesontown, and was planned and developed by the Hutcheson's Hospital Trust in the 19th century as an industrial and residential area. At its heart, in Crown Street, was an imposing Grammar School.

Walk past Gorbals New Park, and at the next gateway, go left and cross the road at the lights. Go under the railway bridge and turn right (into Gorbals Street). Follow the road up past the Citizens' Theatre. The façade dates from 1989, but inside is a gem of an auditorium with horseshoe tiers on iron columns, designed in 1878 by Campbell Douglas.

Continue along the road and cross at the lights. On the right is the complex forming Glasgow's Central Mosque, opened in 1984. The dome is lit at night. On the left is the new Sheriff Courthouse, a fortress-like building which holds no fewer than 21 courtrooms.

At Victoria Bridge, turn right along the riverside walk. Pass Glasgow College of Nautical Studies (where much else is also taught) and at Albert Bridge, turn right on Crown Street. Cross Ballater Street and continue back to the library. The Gorbals was once one of the worst slum areas in Glasgow. It has seen an incredible amount of change since its initial development by Sir George Elphinstone in the 17th century almost as a 'garden suburb' (the name comes from 'gar bhal', an open space). In the late 19th century there was a major influx of Jewish and Irish immigrants and the tenements became seriously overcrowded. Over this long period the population fluctuated from 10,000 to a peak of 70,000. It is now back down to nearer the lower figure.

A major redevelopment started in 1957 when the high-rise apartment blocks were introduced. These have nearly all gone in the latest redesign, but its community spirit has never changed, as this fascinating and unusual walk will have shown you.

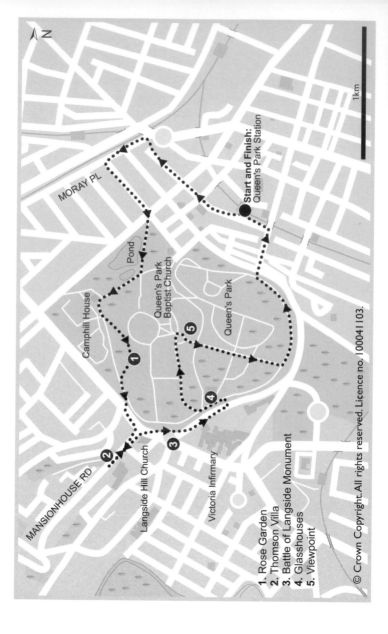

N

MORAY PL

Pond

Camphill House

Queen's Park
Baptist Church

Queen's Park

Start and Finish:
Queen's Park Station

Langside Hill Church

Victoria Infirmary

MANSIONHOUSE RD

1km

1. Rose Garden
2. Thomson Villa
3. Battle of Langside Monument
4. Glasshouses
5. Viewpoint

QUEEN'S PARK

Distance	4km (2.5 miles) circular.
Start and Finish	Queen's Park Station.
Underfoot	Pavement and good paths.
Public transport	Regular train service from Glasgow Central.
Refreshments	Selection of cafes and pubs nearby: café in the Glasshouse.
Toilets	At the Glasshouse.
Opening hours	The Glasshouse is open daily 10.00-16.00 (Friday 10.00-15.00).

A battle, a brilliant architect and a beautiful view: what more could you ask from an urban walk? A look round Glasgow's Queen's Park has all this and much else besides. From the station, turn right and right again into Torrisdale Street, lined with handsome red sandstone tenements. Cross Pollokshaws Road and continue on Nithsdale Road.

At the roundabout, go left into Moray Place. The diversion up here is to see nos 1-10, a superb terrace by the great architect Alexander 'Greek' Thomson. Built in 1858, the design includes chimney pots shaped like lotus flowers and key pattern decoration on the upper frontage. Nos 1 and 10 are larger houses, opening and closing a typically strong Thomson statement.

Turn left on Queen Square, recross Pollokshaws Road and enter the park, with a pond to the right, usually busy with ducks and other birds demanding to be fed. To the left you can see the tall spire of Queen's Park Baptist Church (1875, William Leiper).

Queen's Park was established on ground sold to the city by Neale Thomson of Camphill in 1857 for £30,000. The eminent architect Joseph Paxton was engaged as designer and the park opened in 1862 – without incorporating some of Paxton's more fanciful plans such as a music hall and water gardens. Further land was acquired in 1894. The park is a popular recreation area today. It has many fine mature trees and holds a healthy population of inquisitive squirrels.

At a fork, go right above a smaller pond and continue past Camphill House, a fine early 19th-century mansion which was for a time used as a museum. At the next two forks, keep right, then left, then go

In Queen's Park.

right to reach the Scottish Poetry Rose Garden. The garden contains inscribed stones named for well-known writers from Gavin Douglas (late 15th century) up to the present day. Even the litter bins are dedicated! There are cairns with inscriptions from famous authors, too.

Leave the garden at the cairn to Sorley MacLean and take any of the paths that lead out to Langside Avenue. Turn left and walk up the hill. You can if you wish divert down Mansionhouse Road opposite to see Thomson's intriguing 'double villa' at no 25.

On the right at the top of the hill is the former Langside Hill Church, now a restaurant. It was designed in 1894 by Alexander Skirving, who worked with Thomson, and is in Greco-Roman style. In the centre of the roundabout is the 18m high monument commemorating the Battle of Langside in May 1568, when Mary Queen of Scots' forces lost out to the much superior army of the Regent, Lord Moray. It was a decisive moment, for after it the Queen left Scotland, never to return. The monument, also Skirving's work, dates from 1888. It is topped by a lion with its paw on a cannonball, and there are eagles at each corner of the plinth.

Keep left round the edge of the park, with Victoria Infirmary to the right. It opened in 1890 and was the first proper hospital on the south side of the city. Opposite the Infirmary's imposing entrance, with its

The 1905 Glasshouse.

royal coat of arms, re-enter the park and go sharply left as signed to reach the Glasshouse. This graceful 1905 building contains many fascinating displays of flora and fauna and its heated interior is an antidote to the coldest weather outside. It has a café and toilets.

Leave the Glasshouse, turn right and immediately right again on a path which climbs steadily. At the junction near the top of the hill, go right to the flagpole on its artificial mound. It commands a magnificent view across the city, particularly looking north past the University buildings to the Campsie Fells beyond, with the peak of Dumgoyne prominent. A view indicator is provided – see how many landmarks you can pick out.

From the flagpole walk downhill across a picnic area. At the second junction is a tree planted by the Friends of Kurdistan in memory of Kurds killed by chemical bombing in Halabja, Iraq, in 1988. Continue ahead past the former Pathhead Farmhouse, now the park offices. Walk downhill past bowling greens and turn left on the perimeter path.

Follow this path round to the park's splendid Art Nouveau entrance gates, which date from 1907. Cross the road ahead and the station is a short walk away – or, if you have time, you can continue to explore the park and its many attractions.

WALK 8

37

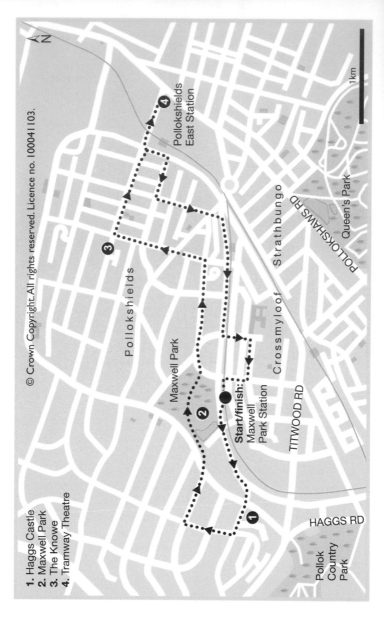

1. Haggs Castle
2. Maxwell Park
3. The Knowe
4. Tramway Theatre

N

Pollokshields

Maxwell Park

The Knowe

Pollokshields East Station

Tramway Theatre

Strathbungo

Queen's Park

POLLOKSHAWS RD

Crossmyloof

TITWOOD RD

Start/finish: Maxwell Park Station

HAGGS RD

Pollok Country Park

1km

POLLOKSHIELDS

Distance	3km (2 miles) circular.
Start and Finish	Maxwell Park Station.
Underfoot	All good paths and pavement.
Public transport	Frequent trains from Glasgow Central.
Refreshments	Reasonable choice in the area. Café at the Tramway.
Toilets	The Tramway (when open).
Opening hours	The Tramway is open 1000-1800 daily, sometimes later.

A walk round Pollokshields provides an opportunity to see one of Glasgow's planned Victorian burghs, in which much of the original housing remains and there are many points of interest. The walk is 'bookended' by a 16th-century tower house and a unique arts venue.

The development of Pollokshields began in 1849 when Sir John Maxwell, the landowner, commissioned the architect David Rhind to draw up plans for the area. Villa development began in 1851 and the construction of the villas (western area) and terraces (eastern area) continued for half a century to give the pattern we still see today, and will follow on this walk.

From the northern side of the station, go left (west) and follow Terregles Avenue. Keep right at the fork and cross St Andrew's Drive. Walk another 50 metres or so. On the left, behind a high wall and shaded by tall trees, is Haggs Castle, by far the oldest building in the area. The earliest parts date from 1585 and were designed as a three-storey L-plan towerhouse. By the 1840s it was ruinous, but it was later restored, and after a variety of uses including a spell as a childrens' museum it has reverted to being a private house.

Continue along Terregles Avenue and take the next right (Albert Drive) noting already the many handsome villas in their own grounds. Take the second right (Springkell Avenue), cross St Andrew's Drive and enter Maxwell Park. This was always designated as open space, gifted to the burgh by Sir John Stirling Maxwell in 1888.

Turn left alongside the pond, which holds a good variety of waterbirds. Keep ahead, then fork right, and at the second junction fork right again to walk out to the ornamental gates at Pollokshields Burgh Hall.

This impressive building was designed in Scots Renaissance style by H.E.Clifford and was completed in 1890. It was fully restored in the 1990s at a cost of over £1 million.

Pass right of the hall, cross the road and turn left. On the right is the semicircle of villas known as the Twelve Apostles, dating from 1894-98. Cross again to walk gently uphill on Glencairn Drive. On the right is Titwood Bowling and Tennis Club, established in 1890. There are particularly good villas opposite at nos 50-52.

Turn left on Shields Road. The tenements at nos 689-709, originally called Olrig Terrace, are finely detailed and spacious inside, as is typical of the period. Many such tenements in Glasgow were sadly demolished in the postwar rush to modernism, but happily this was eventually halted. A good number have survived and are much sought after today.

Further up, nos 553-609 are also excellent. Before that you pass the former 1876 Free Church with its tall tower, now a care home.

At Albert Drive, go briefly left and first left again (Knowehead Gardens) to see The Knowe. This is 'Greek' Thomson's earliest surviving Glasgow villa, completed in 1856, and displays many characteristics of his work in the picturesque Italian style. It was for many years a Salvation Army hostel, but is now again a private residence.

'Greek' Thomson's The Knowe.

Return to Albert Drive and walk down this, one of the most cosmopolitan thoroughfares in the area, with many Asian and Oriental shops and restaurants. Immediately left is Pollokshields Church of Scotland, a Robert Baldie design of 1878. It has beautiful stained glass. Outside is a war memorial based on old Pictish crosses.

On a wall at Herriet Street is a cartouche carrying the original name of Kew Terrace. Few of these survive. Also here is a rare King Edward VIII pillar box.

The rather ornate building on the corner of Darnley Street was built in 1895 as the Glasgow Steam Laundry and Carpet-beating Works and fulfilled this role for over 60 years. It currently houses an electrical company.

Cross Darnley Street to the Tramway Theatre. As the name implies, this was built in 1894 as a tram depot, but since 1989 has been a theatre and arts venue, often breaking new ground in its productions and exhibitions. Behind it is the Hidden or Secret Garden, an open space with plants and sculpture designed as an 'oasis in the city'.

Return to Darnley Street and turn left, then right on Leslie Street. Turn left at Maxwell Square, a pleasant small open space, and walk down Kenmure Street to Nithsdale Road. The tenements on the left at this junction were designed by 'Greek' Thomson.

Pollokshields Church.

Cross the grass to go right, along Terregles Avenue. The tenements at nos 44-84, by H.E.Clifford in 1895, are among the best of their kind.

Go left and then right on Fotheringay Road, where nos 17-57 are also by Clifford. No 33 has a plaque to the pioneer aviator Jim Mollison, the first person to fly the Atlantic solo east to west. Turn left, then right again into Kirkcaldy Road. The Edwardian tenements here have superb tiled (or 'wally') closes which can be seen through the doors. On your left is Titwood cricket ground, where Scotland play some of their international matches.

Turn right on Dolphin Road, then left, back to the station.

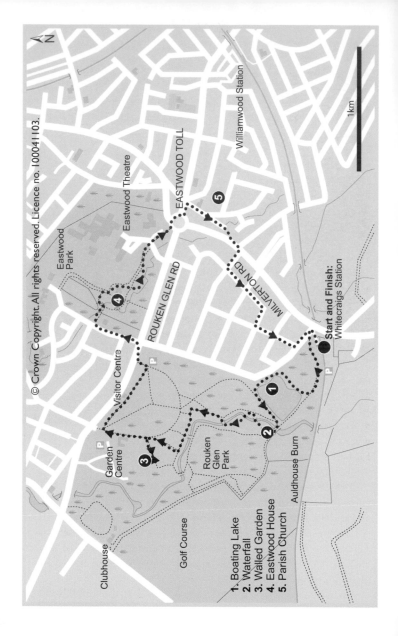

N

1km

Clubhouse

Golf Course

Garden Centre

Visitor Centre

Eastwood Park

Eastwood Theatre

EASTWOOD TOLL

Rouken Glen Park

Auldhouse Burn

ROUKEN GLEN RD

MILVERTON RD

Williamwood Station

Start and Finish: Whitecraigs Station

1. Boating Lake
2. Waterfall
3. Walled Garden
4. Eastwood House
5. Parish Church

ROUKEN GLEN AND EASTWOOD

Distance	5km (3 miles) circular.
Start and Finish	Whitecraigs Station (car park).
Underfoot and access	Pavement and generally good paths. Some sections may be muddy after rain. This walk is not suitable for wheelchairs.
Public transport	Regular train services from Glasgow Central, and buses from the city centre and from East Kilbride.
Refreshments	Café at Rouken Glen.
Toilets	At Rouken Glen.
Opening hours	Rouken Glen Park is open daily. There are many shorter circuits within the park suitable for wheelchairs, accessed from the main entrance on Rouken Glen Road.

This very enjoyable walk explores one of Glasgow's finest parks and the surrounding area. From the station, turn left at the lights and then left again into Rouken Glen Park. The 90-hectare park was gifted to the city by Archibald Cameron-Corbett MP (later Lord Rowallan) in 1906, so has recently celebrated its centenary.

Follow the dirt path uphill, then down to reach the boating pond. Keep right for a circuit of the pond. It is home to ducks and swans, offers boats for hire in summer, and has a seasonal tearoom (Boaters) and toilets. On most Saturday lunchtimes a Model Steamer Club meet here, sailing their beautiful replica ships.

At the end of the long side of the pond after the tearoom, turn right to cross the bridge over the Auldhouse Burn and see the thundering waterfall. Turn right down steps onto the glen path and follow it, with further good views of the falls. You cross the burn three times by footbridges, at one point with a sheer rock face to the right. There are lots of evergreen trees and shrubs, giving a fine display all year round. The little gorge is designated as a Site of Special Scientific Interest for botanical and geological reasons. The mudstone rock contains a variety of fossils.

Keep on the glen path, climbing high above the burn and then passing a wall. Take the first path on the right after this and follow it round to the main broad path through the park. Turn left.

In this area once stood Birkinshaw House (later renamed Thorn-liebank House), a large mansion owned by Walter Crum, a Victorian

The boating pond in Rouken Glen Park.

textile magnate. It was demolished in 1953 and no trace remains. Follow the broad path for about about 150 metres, then go left to the walled garden.

Walk round the garden. From spring to autumn it is a glorious blaze of colour, but even in winter the shrubs and neat box hedges are very pleasing to the eye. Return to the main exit, turn left and left again on the broad path.

Take the second path left, passing the former Cathay Cuisine restaurant. Birkinshaw Cottage here (beyond the stone gateway) was once the home of Madeleine Smith, renowned for her part in a Victorian murder trial (see Walk 3). Keep left for the garden centre. It has a very wide range of plants and other items and has an excellent café and toilets.

Return to the broad path, turn left and then right, still inside the park. Pass the park visitor centre (also the ranger base) and the children's play areas and leave the park at the small car park. Cross the main road at the lights and walk up Wood Farm Road.

Go past the Glen Family Centre and then take a path on the right (past garages) to enter Eastwood Park. Follow the path over a small burn and up to a road. Turn right, then swing left past Eastwood House. This classical mansion is now used for wedding receptions and other events.

At the front door, take the path on the right and then go left, a very pleasant walk beside the burn. Over to the left is the swimming pool and Eastwood Theatre, with St Ninian's School beyond. At the access road for the theatre and council offices (headquarters of East Renfrewshire Council), cross straight over onto a path which leads to gates at Eastwood Toll roundabout.

As the name indicates, this was once a tollgate for vehicles entering or leaving the city. It is now a very busy intersection. Cross two roads with care, going clockwise and heading to the left of the Italian restaurant in a former bank building. Pass a war memorial and walk up Mains Avenue. Up to the left is Giffnock South Church, designed by Stewart and Paterson in late Gothic style and opened in 1929. It has fine stained glass windows.

Continue ahead on the path by the flats and go down steps onto Ayr Road. At the next junction, cross with care into Norwood Drive. Take the first left (Milverton Road), cross Langtree Avenue, curve right and then go left on Torrington Avenue. Turn left along Davieland Road for the short distance back to the station.

The burn through Eastwood Park.

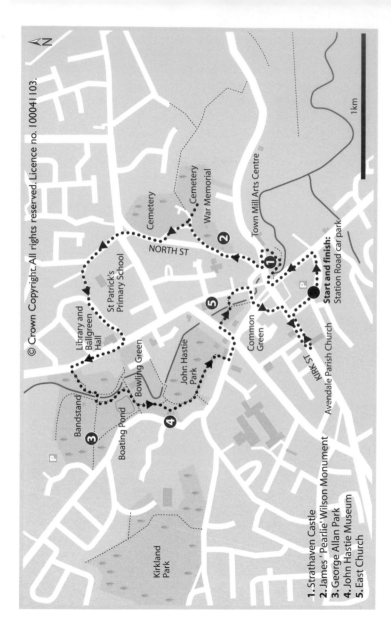

N

1km

Cemetery

Cemetery

War Memorial

NORTH ST

Town Mill Arts Centre

St Patrick's
Primary School

Library and
Ballgreen Hall

Bandstand

Boating Pond

Bowling Green

John Hastie Park

Common Green

KIRK ST

Avendale Parish Church

Kirkland Park

Start and finish:
Station Road car park

1. Strathaven Castle
2. James 'Pearlie' Wilson Monument
3. George Allan Park
4. John Hastie Museum
5. East Church

STRATHAVEN

Distance	3km (2 miles) circular.
Start and Finish	Station Road car park, Strathaven.
Underfoot	Pavement and good paths. Steep climb to the war memorial.
Public transport	Regular bus service from East Kilbride and Hamilton.
Refreshments	Selection of cafes and pubs in the town centre.
Toilets	In Green Street and in Strathaven Park.
Opening hours	John Hastie Museum, open 12.30-16.30 daily, Apr-Sep. Avendale Church is normally open 09.00-12.00 Mon-Fri (not during school holidays).

Historic churches, a powerful castle, a radical rebel and a fine park – a walk round Strathaven will feature all these, and more. From the car park, turn left and follow the road round to the left. Strathaven Central Station was over to the right: the line closed, along with so many others, in the 1960s. Turn left into Todshill Street.

At the foot of the road, go right (cutting the corner) and right again down steps to cross the Powmillon Burn. Go right, then left up a long flight of steps to reach the impressive ruin of Strathaven Castle. Started in 1458 by Sir Andrew Stewart (later Lord Avendale) it was a large fortress five storeys high with 13 turrets.

Anne, Duchess of Hamilton, who was a staunch Royalist, lived here after being ejected from Hamilton Palace by Parliamentary troops in Cromwellian times. After she died in 1716, the castle was used by the townspeople as a church, market place and court, but by the mid-18th century it was ruinous.

Go round the castle to the left and down steps to the road, noting on the right the Town Mill of 1650 (once part of the castle complex). Cross the road and go uphill on Castle Street. Partway up on the right is a monument to James 'Pearly' Wilson. Not only did he invent the knitting machine which first used the purl stitch, he also led the Radical Rising of summer 1820 when aged nearly 60. It was intended to improve social and working conditions for ordinary people, but Wilson was arrested, summarily tried in Glasgow and executed on Glasgow Green (see Walk 2). The monument is on the site of his house.

The boating pond in Strathaven Park.

In this area of Strathaven there was once a host of small weaving sheds. In the mid-19th century the town had 500 handloom weavers operating.

Turn right on the steep lane (Pathfoot) up to the graveyard. Enter and walk up the steps to the War Memorial on Kirkhill. It commands a wonderful panorama of the town and surrounding countryside. The cemetery also holds graves of Covenanting martyrs.

From the cemetery, walk down the roadway and continue along North Street with a large open space to the right. Cross Commercial Road into Overton Road. One of the houses at this junction was originally a bank on Common Green, and was moved here stone by stone in 1891. Where Overton Road bends right, go left on the path past the primary school and continue round into Cochrane Street. Turn left.

Take the path out to Glasgow Road and turn right, past the Ballgreen Hall and Library. A little further on, turn left into George Allan Park. It is named for a local boy who died aged just 13 in 1892. His father, Rev James Allan, provided the money for the park to be laid out in memory of his son. Strathaven Park has many amenities which can be enjoyed. For the walk, cross the burn and go left to the Park Centre (refreshments and toilets). Turn right between the bowling green and boating pond, then left, cross a small burn and curve right. On the right is the John

Hastie Museum. Hastie was a local businessman who left money for the establishment of this part of the park, which is named after him. The museum, which contains much of interest, was opened in 1921.

Continue with playing fields on the left and go right with the path to exit the park opposite the Rankin Church. Dr Rankin, a minister for 56 years, was a prime mover in the Disruption of the Church in 1843.

Turn left, left again at the lights, cross Green Street and take the path across Allison Green. On the left is the handsome East Church, built in 1777 for townsfolk unhappy with the resiting of the Parish Church in Kirk Street. The clock tower was added in 1843. Walk out to Waterside Street and turn right. The renowned Strathaven Toffee was made here from 1904 onwards, and you also pass Alexander Taylor's, a bakery business here since 1820. At the road end is the quaint Bow-Backit (hump-backed) Bridge, which is nearly 300 years old.

Clock tower, Avendale Church.

Turn right and right again through Common Green, which never was a green but was once a marketplace. Turn left on Townhead Street (where the Buck's Head was once a coaching inn) and left again on Thomson Street, past the West Church, the largest in Strathaven. At the end of Thomson Street is the Old Town Hall of 1896, now a Scout and Guide Centre. Turn right to see the Avendale Parish Church. It was built in 1772, but many of the congregation were unhappy with it, as it was on damp ground and had too few seats. So they built the East Church instead! The square steeple carries a fine working clock with the date 1772 at its four corners, and inside the church is a gallery reserved for the family and tenants of the Dukes of Hamilton.

Return to Station Road to end the walk.

WALK 11

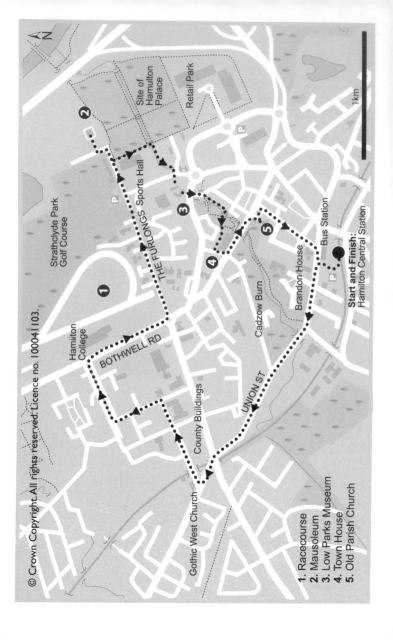

Strathclyde Park
Golf Course

Site of
Hamilton
Palace

Retail Park

① Sports Hall

THE FURLONGS

Hamilton
College

BOTHWELL RD

Gothic West Church

County Buildings

UNION ST

Cadzow Burn

Brandon House

Bus Station

Start and Finish:
Hamilton Central Station

1. Racecourse
2. Mausoleum
3. Low Parks Museum
4. Town House
5. Old Parish Church

1km

N

HAMILTON

Distance	4km (2.5 miles) circular.
Start and Finish	Hamilton Central station (or nearby bus station or car park).
Underfoot	All good paths and pavement.
Public transport	Regular trains from Glasgow Central, and buses from Buchanan Street.
Refreshments	Good choice in town centre.
Toilets	At the bus station and in the Low Parks Museum.
Opening hours	Low Parks Museum is open daily, 10.00-17.00 and is free. There are guided tours of the Mausoleum on Wednesday, Saturday and Sunday at 15.00 (April-September) or 14.00 (October-March).

This walk explores the centre of Hamilton, showing the town's fine architectural heritage and its links with the Dukes of the same name.

Leaving the station or car park, turn left and walk up Brandon Street. At the corner of Auchincampbell Street is an imposing Scots Baronial building, once a humble bakery. To the left you can see Hamilton Grammar School, designed in classical style and opened in 1913.

Continue uphill, now in Union Street, crossing the Cadzow Burn. Cadzow was the original name of the town. On the right is the former Auchingramont Church of 1860, in Decorated Gothic with a fine spire. It is now apartments.

Reach Peacock Cross, named after a Hamilton family who had a smithy here. Continue briefly into Burnbank Road, noting that no 17 was the home of the missionary and African explorer David Livingstone from 1862 until his death in 1873. Turn right into Clydesdale Street, passing the Gothic West Church of 1880.

Cross Douglas Street to pass the headquarters of South Lanarkshire Council. The block, which was modelled on the United Nations HQ in New York, is a listed building. Its 15th floor staff restaurant claims the best view in the county.

Turn left into Beckford Street (noting on the right the 19th-century classical Sheriff Court with its Ionic columns), and then right into Caird Street, and cross the busy road ahead with care. At the junction is a length of richly decorated railings, originally made for Hamilton

Hamilton racecourse.

Palace in 1834. Turn right, walk along to the next roundabout, and turn left down The Furlongs.

Soon you pass the start of the 6-furlong straight at Hamilton racecourse, which still holds regular meetings. In the distance are the Campsie Fells. As you walk down the hill, you can see on the left the loch in Strathclyde Park. Continue into the park to the Hamilton Mausoleum.

This remarkable building, modelled on the tomb of the Emperor Hadrian in Rome, took 15 years to construct and was completed in 1858 at a cost of £33,000 – equivalent to over £1 million today. The original bronze doors, each weighing 760kg and based on the famous Ghiberti doors in Florence, are kept within the chapel, which has the longest echo-time (15 seconds) of any building in Scotland. In the 1920s, due to subsidence caused by old mines, the building sank 5.5m but remarkably suffered little damage.

In this area once stood Hamilton Palace, home of the Dukes of Hamilton from the late 16th century until the 1920s, when it was demolished after also being undermined by subsidence.

Walk back out of the park, turning left on the first path (before the sports hall). Cross the Cadzow Burn and turn right beside it. Curve left with the path past an adventure playground. Turn right at the road and cross to the Low Parks Museum, originally built in 1696 as an inn and now the oldest building within the burgh of Hamilton. The Museum contains much of interest and is well worth a visit. There are displays on local history and industry, the Romans, and the Cameronian Regiment. One of the displays relates to the Blantyre pit disaster of October 1877, when 207 men died.

Turn right past Portwell Mews and cross at the lights. Continue along Portwell and cross the burn into the attractive Cadzow Glen park. Keep left, then, at the next bridge, go right past two sculptures – *Sharing* by Madeleine Wiener and *Floral Trumpets* by Phil Johnson and Co (both 1996).

Walk out to Lower Auchingramont Road and turn left. Turn left again on Cadzow Street past the Town House and Town Hall. The first part of this impressive red sandstone block was opened as a

The Hamilton Mausoleum.

library in 1907. A wall plaque marks the later opening of the Council Chamber in 1914 by King George V. The building has undergone extensive refurbishment and is regularly used for concerts, lectures and meetings.

Cross the Cadzow Burn again. A plaque on the bridge marks the Battle of the Hieton, a covenanting skirmish fought here in 1650. Turn right into Church Place to the Old Parish Church. This was the only church design by the great architect William Adam and dates from 1732. It takes the form of a Greek cross. In front of it is the ancient Netherton Cross, believed to be at least 1000 years old and carved with religious symbols.

Turn right from the church entrance, then right again into Leechlee Road and walk back up to Brandon Street. Note on the corner, outside Brandon House, Mo Farquharson's fine memorial sculpture of two miners, marking the Udston pit disaster of 1887 when 73 miners died.

At the entrance to the bus station is a tall obelisk by Malcolm Robertson covered with horological symbols and marking its position as 55'47"N and 4'25"W. At the end of this satisfying walk you are thus certain of your precise location.

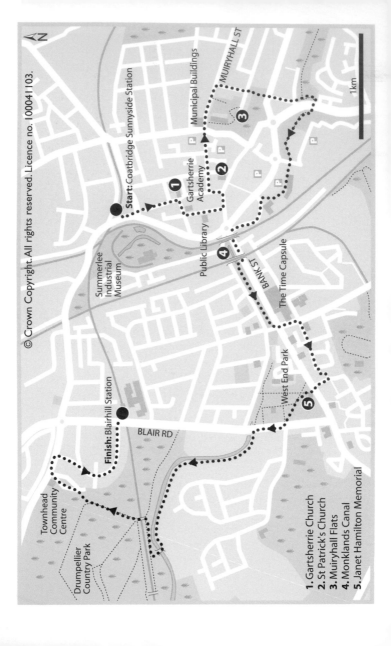

N

Start: Coatbridge Sunnyside Station

Summerlee Industrial Museum

Gartsherrie Academy

Municipal Buildings

MUIRYHALL ST

Public Library

The Time Capsule

BANK ST

West End Park

Finish: Blairhill Station

BLAIR RD

Townhead Community Centre

Drumpellier Country Park

1km

1. Gartsherrie Church
2. St Patrick's Church
3. Muiryhall Flats
4. Monklands Canal
5. Janet Hamilton Memorial

COATBRIDGE

Distance	4km (2.5 miles) linear.
Start and Finish	**Start**: Coatbridge Sunnyside Station. **Finish**: Blairhill Station.
Underfoot	Pavement and generally good paths. Some stretches may be muddy after rain. There are some short, steepish slopes.
Public transport	Frequent train service from Glasgow Queen Street low level.
Refreshments	Good choice in the town centre.
Toilets	In the town centre.
Opening hours	Summerlee Heritage Park in Coatbridge (not on the walk) is a superb museum to the area's industrial heritage. It is open daily 10.00-17.00 (10.00-16.00 Nov-March) and is free. Details from 01236 431261 or *www.northlan.gov.uk*.

'It has the appearance of an immense garden'; 'There is no worse place out of Hell than that neighbourhood'. Both these quotes refer to Coatbridge. The first is from 1799; by the time of the second, only 60 years later, the town was a major industrial centre, with more than 150 furnaces. These have all gone, but reminders of the town's rapid development can still be found.

Turn left over the railway, noting the 1888 datestone on the station building, cross Sunnyside Road and continue up Church Street. At the top is the tall sandstone spire of Gartsherrie Church, built 1839 (churches and factories tended to arrive together as towns developed, the former usually getting the prominent hilltop sites!). The church has a fine 1870 Willis organ.

Turn right on Baird Street, named for James Baird of Gartsherrie (1802-76), one of the principal industrialists, and pass Gartsherrie Academy, built by the Bairds for their workers' children in 1845 – an enlightened act for the time. It is now converted to housing. Turn left down Academy Street, passing the Library (1905, Alexander Cullen) and left along Main Street.

Walk along to St Patrick's Church, a Pugin design of 1896 built to cater for the large Irish workforce here at the time, turn left on St John Street and right on Muiryhall Street. Cross Dunbeth Street at the lights, noting on the left McGregor Mitchell's powerful Municipal Buildings of 1894, with statues of Justice and Industry, and continue

WALK 13

55

Gartsherrie Church.

uphill on Muiryhall Street East. Turn right on Jackson Street past the Clifton Church (1874, Hugh McLure), with its distinctive tower. Walk downhill, with the vast Muiryhall flats (J.S.Stewart, 1931-34) on one side and Jackson Court (1960s) on the other.

Continue downhill on a path, and cross the road at the lights. If you look left you may see the floodlights at Cliftonville, the ground of Albion Rovers FC. Continue down in the same direction across Coatbank Way then follow NCR75 cycleway signs up the ramp and across the footbridge.

On the far side turn right and then left. Fork left (still with NCR75), cross the road and walk along the side of the Asda car park past the Health Centre. Keep left at the footbridge into Whittington Street, past the police station. Continue into Ellis Street. On the corner is the former Lanarkshire Coalmasters' Association Rescue Station of 1914, nicely refurbished as the Fountain Business Centre.

Turn left on Bank Street, cross the road at the lights and walk down to the path beside a short section of the former Monklands Canal, once a major artery for industry here. Much of the heavy industry was sited along the canal. Bairds alone had over 50 furnaces producing 300,000 tons of iron a year and employing 10,000 men and boys, mostly in terrible conditions. James Baird was a substantial philanthropist, giving more than £500,000 to the church.

On the right is Watermans Bar, in the former Central Station of 1899. Keep on the path. Further along on the right is the former Coatbridge Market, with a powerful sculpture of a bull's head. On the left is the Time Capsule leisure centre.

Take the next path left and cross into Dundyvan Road. Turn right on Buchanan Street. On the corner is St Augustine's RC Church, a typically strong Pugin design of 1907 in red sandstone. Keep ahead to Loch Broom Crescent and then take a narrow fenced path to Langloan Street. Turn right.

Cross the main road to the Janet Hamilton Memorial. She was a well-known local poet who died in 1873. It is reported that when the memorial was unveiled in 1880, there was a crowd of 20,000 present. Turn right, then left into West End Park and follow the path across the park. Turn right on Blair Road. At the bridge, go down steps on the left to the path alongside the old canal.

This is a pleasant walk for about 800m, and you may see swans and other waterbirds. Keep with the main path as it rises and then cross the canal by a bridge, into Drumpellier Country Park, a very large open space. Turn right and then go left under the railway.

Turn immediately right on a small rough path with football pitches to the left and broom bushes to the right. Follow this path along, keep right and walk out to the road. Turn left, up past the Community Centre. Turn right on Townhead Road and first right on Espieside Crescent. Follow this road all the way round until you see Blairhill Station across the road ahead of you.

Coatbridge today is neither garden nor Hell, but has settled into a new life, with plenty for the inquiring visitor to discover.

The Monklands Canal.

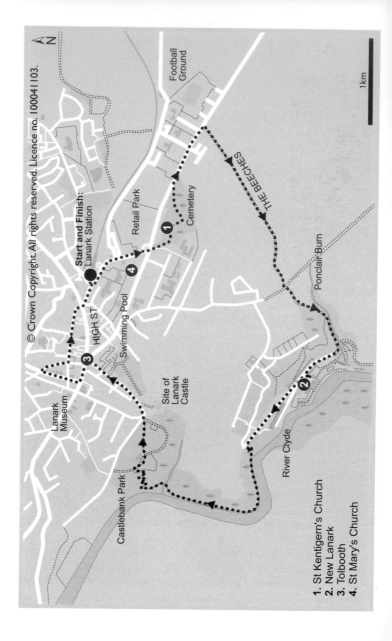

N

Start and Finish: Lanark Station

Football Ground

Cemetery

Retail Park

1

4

HIGH ST

Swimming Pool

THE BEECHES

Ponclair Burn

Lanark Museum

3

Site of Lanark Castle

Castlebank Park

2

River Clyde

1km

1. St Kentigern's Church
2. New Lanark
3. Tolbooth
4. St Mary's Church

LANARK AND NEW LANARK

Distance	6km (4 miles) circular.
Start and Finish	Lanark Railway Station.
Underfoot	Pavement and generally good paths. Steep climb up to Castlebank Park.
Public transport	Regular train services from Glasgow Central low level.
Refreshments	Selection of cafes and pubs in the town centre. Restaurant at New Lanark.
Toilets	At the start and at New Lanark.
Opening hours	New Lanark is open daily all year, Jun-Aug 10.30-17.00, Sep-May 11.00-17.00. Further details from 01555 665738 or *www. newlanark.org.* .

This is one of the longer walks in the book, but offers both fine scenery and interesting history. From the station, cross the road at the lights and turn left. Continue down to the roundabout with the new retail park on the left. It is on the site of the Auction Mart, and the octagonal auction building, dating from 1867, has been retained.

Cross the first road at the roundabout, then take the entry ahead into the cemetery. Ahead of you as you enter is the ruin of the old St Kentigern's Church, its foundation dating back to the 12th century. Legend states that William Wallace married Marion Braidfute here – you may have noticed that the retail park is named after her.

Follow the path to the left, curve right, then go left through a gateway, and then right to the large mausoleum. Continue for a short distance to the tall Covenanters' Monument commemorating many men who had to flee the area because of their religious beliefs. Some died: others ended up in colonies such as Australia and Canada.

Return past the mausoleum, turn right and fork left to the main path. Go right at the central area with seats, then left to find the unusual monument (a large block of Glen Etive granite) in memory of Brian Seymour, 'adventurer', who died in 1989 aged just 22.

Head for the far right-hand corner, leave the cemetery and continue along Hyndford Road, noting the fine gateway of the former Lady Hozier Convalescent Home. It was a gift to the town by Sir William Hozier in memory of his wife and was opened in 1893. An interesting

New Lanark and the river.

historical note is that Sir William's niece Clementine later married Sir Winston Churchill.

At the end of the wall, turn right down the old right of way path known as The Beeches. It formerly commanded wide views in both directions. There is still a big sweep of country with Tinto prominent to the left, but on the right is now a large new housing estate, whose two access roads you cross.

Continue down the path, crossing a lane and now on a narrow stony path. Reach another lane and swing right to reach the large group of buildings at New Lanark. This is a truly remarkable place. There is not space to describe it in full here, but happily, much of the 'industrial village' complex has survived, enabling us to appreciate the extraordinary vision of David Dale and Robert Owen in setting it up at a time (the late 18th century) when working conditions generally were extremely poor. Here, the workers had light and space and there were schools for the children (including the world's first nursery school), free health care and recreational facilities as well. Much of the complex can be explored: start at the excellent Visitor Centre. New Lanark is registered by UNESCO as a World Heritage Site.

When you are ready to leave, take the access road that rises steadily, passing Robert Owen's house. Just before the road bends sharply back right, go left on a path which leads down towards the Clyde. This path was made as part of the Clyde Walkway in 1995, but the Walkway has since been moved to the other side of the river.

One of the mills at New Lanark.

The path reaches a viewpoint with a superb panorama of New Lanark and the river. Continue down a long flight of steps almost to river level. This is a beautiful stretch of the path, so enjoy it as there is some hard work to come! There is usually a good variety of birdlife and you may see squirrels in the trees.

Cross a burn by a footbridge and then start climbing steadily. The path reaches a series of zig-zags which haul you up in time to Castlebank Park. At the main path in the park, turn right past Castlebank House. There is a terraced garden on the right which you can explore if you wish. The house dates back to the late 18th century. It was sold to the then town council in 1951 and is now divided into flats.

From the house take the rising path that leads up to the park gates. Turn right, then left into Castlegate. You pass (on your right) the site of the original Lanark Castle. It was established in the 12th century, and there is no doubt that Wallace was here in 1297 and attacked the Sheriff of Lanark. Robert the Bruce held court at the castle in 1321, but not long after that it became disused, and nothing now remains.

Walk up Castlegate. Over to the left, with its entrance in Friar's Lane, is Castlepark, a house designed in Japanese style by the eccentric William Leiper. Further up, the large building between Castlegate and Broomgate was the Broomgate Institute, built in 1838 as a school for poor children. Near the top of Castlegate is a plaque marking the supposed site of William Wallace's house.

At the Tolbooth you reach the historic heart of Lanark, including St Nicholas' Parish Church with its large statue of Wallace, and the Tolbooth. The latter dates from 1778, and was originally three storeys high, but due to the raising of the High Street over the years, only two storeys are now visible.

WALK 14

St Nicholas Church with its statue of Wallace.

The church is of the same period (1774) and has a 6-stage steeple. This notable local landmark holds the town bell, which dates back to the 12th century. The statue of Wallace, by Robert Forrest, dates from 1822, and is prominent in the Lanimer celebrations held in Lanark each June. Lanimers were the original burgesses of the town and part of their duties was to ride the marches, or boundaries, each year. This was the basis of Lanimer Day (now Week), which has gradually developed into a major festival of celebrations and events.

Cross the road and turn left. Turn right on Hope Street. It dates from 1829 and extended the town away from the High Street. On the corner is the 1855 Meal Market, and a little further along is the Lindsay Institute, built of Northumberland ashlar in 1914 with funds provided by Charles Lindsay.

St Kentigern's Church, now converted to offices and flats, dates from 1884 and has a spire rising to over 40 metres. Opposite is the Sheriff Court, added to the County Buildings in 1868 and still in use today.

At Christ Church, turn sharp right along Greenside Lane. Several of its houses have 'thackstones' beneath the chimneys, indicating that they were once thatched. At the junction (car park opposite) turn left into North Vennel. This was originally a lane outside the town walls, and was the site of many small businesses and workshops.

Follow North Vennel along past Tesco's, and where the roadway ends, swing right to regain the High Street. Turn left and then fork right at the lights to return to the station, as you do so crossing South Vennel, another reminder of Lanark's original street pattern.

Over on the right is St Mary's Church, rebuilt 1908-10 after a fire destroyed the previous church. It is in Gothic revival style and has a lovely slender spire and a richly decorated interior.

WALK 14

BIGGAR

Distance	3km (2 miles) circular.
Start and Finish	High Street, Biggar.
Underfoot	Good paths and pavement.
Public transport	Reasonable bus services from Lanark and Edinburgh.
Refreshments	Good choice in town centre. Tearoom at the park.
Toilets	In John Street and at the Public Park.
Opening hours	Gladstone Court and the Moat Park Heritage Centre: May-Sep Mon-Sat 11.00-16.30, Sun 14.00-16.30. Gasworks Museum: Jun-Sep daily 14.00-17.00. Greenhill: Sat/Sun only, 14.00-16.30. For details of the Puppet Theatre phone 01899 220631 or go to www.purvespuppets.com.

Biggar is a busy and thriving community, and a walk around the town and its environs reveals a surprising range of interesting places.

From the broad High Street, walk south down John Street. On the corner is the former Corn Exchange (1860), now a theatre. High on its rear wall, a rather curious place to find such a relic, is a fragment of the town's old Mercat Cross.

Turn left on South Back Road and follow it along, passing several attractive cottages. Notice the very narrow Smiddy's Close on the left, typical of the myriad lanes that once linked main thoroughfares with other parts of towns such as Biggar.

Turn right on Broughton Road and take the third right (Park Road). On the right is the unusual Puppet Theatre, which has been entertaining kids of all ages since 1970. Continue along the road with fine views of the hills ahead. Reach a golf course on the right and then Biggar Public Park, which has a range of facilities including a campsite, tennis, football pitch, children's playground and a tearoom. Turn right by the pretty pond, which usually holds ducks and swans.

At the end of the pond continue on the track, crossing the Biggar Burn. On the left is the embankment of the former Symington, Biggar and Broughton Railway, opened in 1860 and closed to passenger traffic in 1950. It must have been a beautiful run.

Just after the next bridge over the burn, turn left on a path (right of way sign) and walk beside the burn, across the golf course. Please give

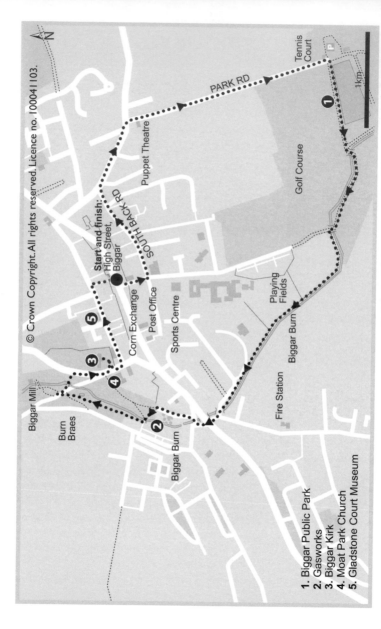

N

Tennis Court

PARK RD

Puppet Theatre

SOUTH BACK RD

Golf Course

Start and finish:
High Street,
Biggar

Corn Exchange

Post Office

Sports Centre

Playing Fields

Fire Station

Biggar Burn

Biggar Mill

Burn Braes

Biggar Burn

1km

1. Biggar Public Park
2. Gasworks
3. Biggar Kirk
4. Moat Park Church
5. Gladstone Court Museum

Biggar Burn and the Cadger's Brig.

way if golfers are playing across your line. The path swings right, with fine views towards Tinto Hill.

Continue beside the little burn, back towards the town, passing the site of the new school. Follow the path until it joins a road, cross Station Road, and go right, across High Street into Park Place, to cross the old Cadger's Brig. Legend associates this wee bridge with William Wallace, but it is unlikely to be that ancient. It gets its name from the cadgers, or pedlars, who crossed it bringing goods for sale into the town market.

Turn into Gas Works Road. On the left is the former Gasworks, opened in 1836. It closed in 1973 when mains gas became available and is now the only remaining coal gas plant in Scotland. It is run as an outstation of the Royal Museum of Scotland and is open to visitors in summer. A curious medical footnote is that when the gas purifiers were being cleaned, children with whooping cough were brought here to inhale the sulphur.

WALK 15

Enter the delightful park of Burn Braes. Go left to cross a foot-bridge over the burn and immediately turn right on a path. Stay close to the burn. Over to the right is the Motte Knowe, a man-made tree-clad mound which once, long ago, held a castle.

Walk to the end of the park to see on the left Biggar Mill, once owned by the Free Church, and on the right the handsome 17th-century Greenhill Farmhouse. It was rebuilt on this site having been dismantled at Wiston, several miles away, and is now partly a museum devoted to the Covenanters.

Go back to recross the burn at the bridge next to the ford. Walk up the hill to Kirkstyle and turn right. On the left is Biggar Kirk, parts of which date back to 1545. The church has beautiful stained glass, in the porch is a carved medieval tombstone, and the graveyard holds many interesting stones.

The MacDiarmid plaque.

Opposite the kirk is the former Moat Park Church (1865), now a Heritage Centre relating the history of the town and the surrounding area of Upper Clydesdale and Tweeddale. It is well worth a visit.

Turn left into North Back Road. Along here is Gladstone Court Museum, with its fine old shops of yesteryear, including a chemist's and a cobbler's. It also has railway memorabilia and an Albion Dogcart car dating from 1902. Albion cars were made near Biggar from 1899 by Thomas Murray.

From the museum, walk back a little way and turn down Brownlie Close, back to the High Street. As you do so, note the large plaque to Hugh MacDiarmid on the house wall opposite. The inscription reads "let the lesson be, to be yersels and to mak that worth bein".

The High Street has handsome buildings reflecting the growth of Biggar in Victorian times. The wide range of excellent individual shops clearly shows that, while amply acknowledging its rich past, Biggar moves with the times and looks forward to the future with confidence.

HELENSBURGH

Distance	5.5km (3.5 miles) circular.
Start and Finish	Helensburgh Central Station.
Underfoot	Pavement and good paths. No special footwear needed.
Public transport	Regular trains from Glasgow Queen Street low level.
Refreshments	Reasonable choice in Helensburgh.
Toilets	At the pier or at Hill House (if open).
Opening hours	The Hill House is open 1 Apr-31 Oct, daily 13.30-17.30 (further details: 0844 493 2208 or *www.nts.org.uk*). The West Kirk is usually open 09.00-17.00.
Further information	A leaflet showing the path network is available at the Tourist Information Centre.

Just over 100 years ago, in 1904, the Blackie family moved in to their new home, overlooking the Clyde at the upper edge of Helensburgh. Today, The Hill House is world-famous as a marvel of integrated design and one of Charles Rennie Mackintosh's finest achievements. It is the centrepiece of this walk, and recent footpath development enables a scenic approach to the house. Before (and indeed after) that, Helensburgh has much else to offer.

From the station, exit to Sinclair Street, cross and continue along West Princes Street into Colquhoun Square, named for Sir James Colquhoun of Luss, who developed the town (to which he gave his wife's name) in the 18th century. Walk round the square anti-clockwise. Buildings of note here include the striking 1893 Post Office and J. & W. Hay's 1853 West Kirk. It has a beautiful interior, with memorial windows dedicated to John Logie Baird and Andrew Bonar Law, who was Prime Minister in 1922-23. The 1861 classical Bank of Scotland building has an interesting 1980s pyramidal extension.

Head down James Street (which features a 1913 former picture-house, now a bar) to the Esplanade, and the slender monument to Henry Bell. He was the town's first Provost and an innovative marine engineer. His *Comet*, launched in 1812, was the first passenger-carrying steamship in Europe. Bell died in Helensburgh in 1830. We meet him again in Port Glasgow, where the *Comet* was launched (Walk 18).

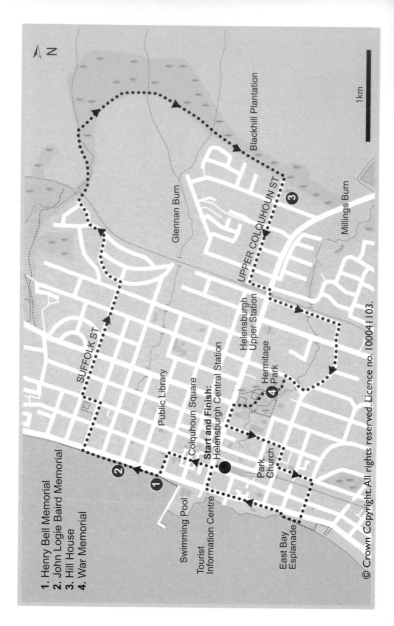

1. Henry Bell Memorial
2. John Logie Baird Memorial
3. Hill House
4. War Memorial

SUFFOLK ST

UPPER COLQUHOUN ST

Blackhill Plantation

Glennan Burn

Millings Burn

Public Library

Helensburgh Upper Station

Colquhoun Square

Hermitage Park

Start and Finish:
Helensburgh Central Station

Swimming Pool

Tourist
Information Centre

Park
Church

East Bay
Esplanade

© Crown Copyright. All rights reserved. Licence no. 100041103.

1km

N

On the left is the pier. This was once a busy centre for pleasure cruisers, and the *Waverley* still calls in from time to time. Ferries leave for Kilcreggan and Gourock. There is a lovely view to the Rosneath Peninsula, seen across the mouth of the Gare Loch.

Walk away from the pier, enjoying the sea air and the expansive views, until you reach a bust of John Logie Baird. Baird, a Helensburgh man, was the prime early developer of television; what on earth would he think of today's programmes?

Continue to Glasgow Street and turn right. Take the second left, King Street, and the next right, Suffolk Street. As you start to climb you can appreciate the way Helensburgh is laid out with a grid pattern of spacious streets, to a design by Charles Ross. Most of the town is exactly twice as old as The Hill House. With the development of steamships and later the railway, it became a popular weekend resort for Glaswe

John Logie Baird, the inventor of television.

gians and a place for the more successful of them to live. John Logie Baird was born in a house on Suffolk Street.

Continue all the way up across Queen Street, then turn left on Barclay Drive (looking back here there is a good view across the Clyde). Turn left again on Macleod Drive and right on Paterson Drive. At its end continue on the track under the railway (signed for The Hill House).

The track climbs steadily, swinging left twice. As it bends left again, continue ahead on a path into the woods (yellow arrow). This is part of an extensive network of paths around Helensburgh. Follow the attractive path through the trees, across a small burn, until it reaches a gap in the wall at a field edge. Follow the path with a drystone dyke on your right. The view from here is superb.

The path meanders along the edge of Blackhill Plantation, through bracken and birch trees, and passing some fine old oaks.

It is well surfaced and level and makes a very pleasant walk. Wild flowers include marsh orchids. Eventually the path swings right to reach the car park for The Hill House.

The house, owned by the National Trust for Scotland since 1982, was commissioned in 1902 by the publisher Walter Blackie, who asked Mackintosh to design not just the building but all the furniture, fittings and decoration. The result is magnificent, fully justifying Blackie's boldness and reflecting Mackintosh's genius. A tour is strongly recommended, and you should also visit the beautiful garden, again largely designed by CRM.

On leaving the house, walk down Upper Colquhoun Street, noting the elegant Mackintosh-style lamp-posts. Turn left at its end, cross the railway at Helensburgh Upper Station (from where you can catch a train to Fort William, Oban or Mallaig) and turn left (East Rossdhu Drive). Follow the road as it bends right and becomes Charlotte Street, heading downhill towards the river.

The Hill House.

Turn right at the island along Victoria Road and then go left into Hermitage Park, a very attractive open space. Walk down between high hedges, then swing right. On the right is the town's elaborate war memorial, in an enclosure with inscribed gates. Pass tennis courts and then fork right to exit into Sinclair Street. Turn left past the ornate Victoria Halls.

Turn left into East Argyle Street and right on Charlotte Street past Park Church with its graceful spire. Cross the railway and turn left along East Princes Street. Turn right on Glenfinlas Street down to the

Overlooking the Gare Loch from Helensburgh.

East Esplanade. On display here is a flywheel from the *Comet*. Turn right along the waterfront, heading for the Italianate tower of the old parish church, designed by Charles Wilson in 1846. It now houses the Tourist Information Centre.

Turn right up Sinclair Street to return to the station. No 40 is an elegant sandstone building designed in 1894 by Honeyman and Keppie, for whom Mackintosh worked for a time. Might he have had some influence on the design of this building? We can only speculate as we end our tour of Helensburgh.

Walter Blackie must have made the short journey down to the station many times, happy in the knowledge that he would return to his wonderful home later in the day.

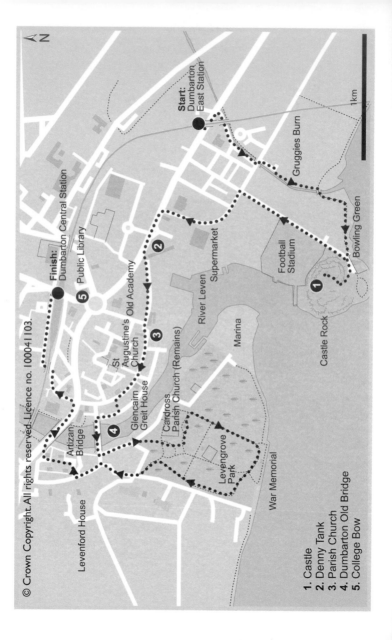

Start: Dumbarton East Station

Gruggies Burn

Bowling Green

Football Stadium

Castle Rock

Supermarket

River Leven

Marina

2

3

St Augustine's Old Academy Church

Glencairn Greit House

Cardross Parish Church (Remains)

Artizan Bridge

4

Levenford House

War Memorial

Levengrove Park

Public Library

Finish: Dumbarton Central Station

5

1km

1. Castle
2. Denny Tank
3. Parish Church
4. Dumbarton Old Bridge
5. College Bow

DUMBARTON

Distance	5km (3 miles) linear.
Start and Finish	**Start**: Dumbarton East station. **Finish**: Dumbarton Central station.
Underfoot	All good paths and pavement.
Public transport	Frequent trains from Glasgow Queen Street low level.
Refreshments	Reasonable choice in town centre. Café at the Denny Tank.
Toilets	At the old bridge and at the visitor attractions (if open).
Opening hours	Dumbarton Castle (Historic Scotland) Apr-Sep daily 09.30-16.45, Oct-Mar daily 10.00-16.00. Denny Ship Tank open Mon-Sat 10.00-16.00.

Dumbarton is *Dun Breatann*, the fort of the Britons, and was once the capital of the ancient kingdom of Strathclyde. It has a very long history and this tour also provides enjoyable riverside walking.

Leaving the station, turn left and take the first right (Buchanan Street). Castle Rock is clear ahead, and the little Gruggies Burn flows by on the left. At the road junction, turn left over the burn and then right on a spur road serving factories. At the gate, look for an almost hidden path on the right with an old signpost to Dumbarton Foreshore.

This path appears unpromising at first, but it has a good surface, and follows the burn down. Cross the footbridge and continue down to the shore. There are great views left upriver past the Erskine Bridge and right to the castle on its towering rock. There is usually plenty of birdlife too.

Go right, along the path towards the castle. At its foot is the Rock Bowling Club, in an amazing location. Walk up the steps to the castle entrance. There has been a fortification here for 1500 years (its continuous history is said to be the longest in Britain), and up to the 11th century this was the centre of the kingdom of Strathclyde. Mary, Queen of Scots was kept safe here as a small child in 1548 until she could be taken to France. It was garrisoned until World War 2; most of the buildings we see today are 18th-century. The long and extraordinarily diverse history of the castle is very well detailed on interpretive panels and in its guidebook.

View over Dumbarton from the Castle.

A visit is strongly recommended and, as might be expected, the view from the top – reached by climbing over 500 steps! – is superb, taking in not just the Clyde in both directions and the town and River Leven, but also looking north to Ben Lomond and beyond.

Below the castle is a grass area with seats, a great place for a picnic. To continue the walk, go up Castle Road, passing the ground of Dumbarton FC, known as 'the Sons'. Take the first left (Leven Street) and curve right, past the supermarket. Turn left at the main road, go ahead at the roundabout (passing an unusual metal sculpture of a shipworker), and then first left on Castle Street.

Near the junction is a maritime museum holding the Denny Tank. This unglamorous structure, holding 1.75 million litres of water, was the world's first experimental tank for ship models, and dates from 1882. It is an A-listed building because of its importance to maritime development. Visitors can try their hand with a model. Outside is the engine from the PS *Leven*, designed by Robert Napier in 1824 and built in Dumbarton.

Continue past the former Dumbarton Distillery, now largely demolished as part of a major renovation project. At the start of the High Street is the Parish Church, also A-listed and dating from 1811. Its design is classically simple rather than ornate.

Turn right briefly into Church Street to see the elaborate frontage of the Old Academy, once the Burgh Hall and Library, designed in 1865 by William Leiper. The building was seriously damaged by fire in 1976 and its future is uncertain.

Return to the High Street and turn right. As with many other towns, Dumbarton's centre has not always been sympathetically treated, but there are still some interesting buildings. St Augustine's Episcopal Church was designed by Sir Robert Rowand Anderson in 1873 and is A-listed, with a superb interior which would no doubt have been appreciated by Charles Rennie Mackintosh, who was married to Margaret MacDonald here in 1899. Note on the left the fine Art Deco fronts of both Burton's and Woolworth's, dating from the 1930s. Between them is Glencairn Greit House, the oldest building in Dumbarton. It dates from 1623 and was the town house of the Earls of Glencairn. The town's Mercat Cross once stood outside it, and a plaque (unveiled in 1996 by a descendant of the poet) records a visit by Robert Burns in 1787.

Walk under the building through the Quay Pend, a good example of an old vennel linking the High Street and the river. Turn right and walk along to Dumbarton Old Bridge, a fine 5-arch structure by John Brown dating from 1765. Cross the bridge, enjoying the views up the River Leven.

On the far side, turn left on Woodyard Road. At the junction with Levenford Terrace take the path ahead into Levengrove Park, a large open space which was once the country estate of the industrialist John Dixon (of Dixon's Blazes fame in Glasgow – see Walk 7). Cross a junction of paths and then go left to see the scant remains of the former Cardross Parish Church.

Turn right on the next main path and walk down to the Clyde. Turn right past the war memorial. There are good views across the

Municipal Buildings and the College Bow Arch.

river to Langbank. Keep inside the park and go right, on the perimeter path, then left to exit by the main gates. Turn right, downhill (Clydeshore Road), then left along West Bridgend. There are large houses here built for ship-owners in Victorian times. One of the finest, up on the left, is Levenford House, a Scots Baronial mansion of 1853 designed by J.T.Rochead, and currently used as council offices.

Pass the West Kirk and at the main road, opposite Dalreoch station, turn right and cross the Artizan Bridge, opened in 1974. Take the first left (Station Road), and then go left again under the railway on Bankend Road, which immediately swings right. Pass the station and turn right on Townend. On the left is Dumbarton Common. Once a lagoon, it was secured as a public open space as recently as 1996.

Walk down towards the roundabout. On the right are the Municipal Buildings (James Thomson, 1904) in Scots Baronial style. Outside them is a statue of Dr Peter Denny and also the College Bow arch, all that remains of the 15th-century Church of St Mary. To the left is the public library, gifted in 1909 by Andrew Carnegie.

Return to Station Road and turn left to Dumbarton Central station – itself a listed building dating from 1896 – to end the walk.

PORT GLASGOW

Distance	5km (3 miles) circular.
Start and Finish	Port Glasgow Station.
Underfoot	All good paths and pavement. One long, steady climb.
Refreshments	Reasonable choice in Port Glasgow.
Public transport	Regular train service from Glasgow Central.
Toilets	Opposite the bus station and at Newark Castle (if open).
Opening hours	Newark Castle is open daily, 09.30-18.30, April to September. There is more about Port Glasgow on the town's community website, *www.portglasgow4u.co.uk*.

This enjoyable walk includes Scotland's first steamship, a superb castle and gorgeous views, so has plenty to offer. From the station, walk down John Wood Street (named for the *Comet's* builder) and turn left into Bay Street. On the right is the fine Town Building and Library, designed in 1815 by David Hamilton. The 60m steeple is topped by a copper weathervane of a fully rigged ship.

Continue into Fore Street and once past the bus station, go left on Scarlow Street. On the left is the former Town Hall. Inside it is a large mural showing river scenes, painted by a local art teacher, James Watt, in 1964 for the opening of the building. Just past the Town Hall is St John's RC Church, dating to 1854.

Cross the road to see the splendid replica of the *Comet*, built in 1962 to mark the 150th anniversary of the launch of Henry Bell's pioneering steamship, here in Port Glasgow. Just beyond it is an information board and another model, on a wall stone. John Wood Snr died during the construction of the vessel in late 1811 and his son, also John, completed the task for the launch in July 1812. On her maiden voyage from Glasgow to Greenock, two gentlemen who landed at Bowling were the first people in Britain to pay a fare for a steamship ride.

The area beyond the model has been redeveloped for a major supermarket and the road pattern changed, and it is not easy to get to the shore. Go right of the roundabout, cross the A8 with great care and walk down Anderson Street, bending left to reach Steamboat Quay. Turn right along the waterfront past the old Perch Lighthouse. There

WALK 18

77

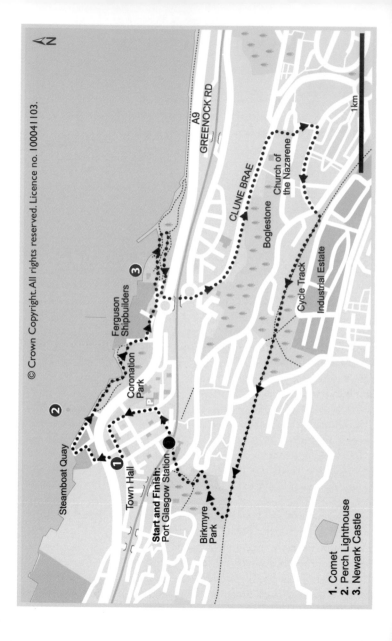

N

2 Steamboat Quay

Town Hall

1

Ferguson Shipbuilders

3

Coronation Park

P

A9 GREENOCK RD

CLUNE BRAE

Boglestone

Church of the Nazarene

Cycle Track

Industrial Estate

Start and Finish: Port Glasgow Station

Birkmyre Park

1km

1. Comet
2. Perch Lighthouse
3. Newark Castle

is a superb view across the Clyde to Helensburgh and beyond to the hills of Cowal, and upriver to Dumbarton Rock.

Continue into Coronation Park. Keep close to the shore round the inlet and slipway, then turn right to reach the road at Fergusons' Shipyard (Newark Quay). Across the A8 you can see the former Gourock Ropeworks building, now converted to flats. Rope

The Comet.

was made in Port Glasgow from the mid-18th century onwards.

Follow the road past the Fire Station, and at the roundabout, take the access road for Newark Castle. As you do so, you pass Fergusons' gates and inside can see the dock where ships are still Clyde-built.

Walk round to the castle. Now in the care of Historic Scotland, Newark is a typical fortified tower, parts of which are late 15th century, and was a stronghold of the Maxwell family. It is remarkably complete and is well worth a visit. The name (repeated elsewhere in Scotland) simply means 'the new work'. The castle was extensively redeveloped in the late 16th and early 17th century by Sir Patrick Maxwell. He carved the date 1597 and a monogram with his own and his wife's initials over the main doorway.

Patrick Maxwell was a powerful and ruthless man and despite the message over the door ('the blessings of God be herein'), was not known for his charity. He killed several of his rival lairds and treated his long-suffering wife Margaret, who bore him 16 children, abominably. He did however refurbish the castle to a high standard, as you can see in the Great Hall with its magnificent fireplace. The castle's excellent guidebook will tell you much more.

Past the castle is Newark Castle Park, which provides an enjoyable stroll. Take any of the paths to walk round the park. Offshore here there were formerly large 'timber ponds' where wood was held before being loaded onto ships for export.

The town developed in the 17th century because it was difficult to keep a dredged channel further upriver nearer to the centre of Glasgow.

WALK 18

79

Newark Castle.

It was originally called New Port Glasgow, but over time the 'New' was dropped. It was at one time the major outlet for timber in the west of Scotland.

Go back towards the roundabout and cross the road, again with care, just east of it. Pass under the railway and at the second roundabout, keep right to go up Clune Brae. This is a steady climb so take your time. At the top of this brae (not on the walk) is the Boglestone, a black granite boulder said to have supernatural powers.

Pass the Church of the Nazarene (a new building) and at the end of the wall, go right up a long flight of steps, continuing all the way up to Cardross Avenue. Turn left and keep right past the schools. Turn right on Bridgend Avenue, follow this road to its end and turn right on the cyclepath (signed 'Gourock 6'). This is part of the NCR75 route which crosses Scotland.

At first the path is enclosed, but the views soon open out and it is a very pleasant walk. At one point you can enjoy a great view of the Greenock Container Port through an unusual 'porthole' sculpture. Cross a footbridge and continue over a road, along the path which is now following an old railway line. There are lovely wild flowers here in spring and summer. In about another 500 metres, take the path on the right leading sharply back and downhill into Birkmyre Park.

Follow the path down, go right across a bridge, then left on the main path, which curves further left. Then go right, down steps to Highholm Avenue. Cross the road and head for the path under the railway. The entry to the station is just on the right before the bridge.

GREENOCK

Distance	5km (3 miles) linear.
Start and Finish	**Start**: Greenock West Station. **Finish**: Greenock Central Station.
Underfoot	Pavement and good paths. Steady climb at the start.
Public transport	Regular train service from Glasgow Central.
Refreshments	Selection of cafes and pubs in the town centre.
Toilets	Oak Mall shopping centre.
Opening hours	Greenock Cemetery is open 08.00-20.00 Apr-Sep, 08.00-18.00 Oct-Mar. The McLean Museum is open Mon-Sat 10.00-17.00 and is free.

Greenock has a surprising amount to offer, and this walk takes in an exceptionally fine viewpoint as well as many interesting buildings and monuments.

From Greenock West Station, cross two roads and turn right along Orangefield. On the left is St Patrick's RC Church, a typically powerful red-brick design by Antonio Coia. Over the doors is a large stone sculpture of St Patrick blessing a child, by Archibald Dawson.

Take the first turning right, cross Inverkip Road and enter the cemetery. Follow the access road up the hill. Where the road turns right to the Crematorium, go slightly right on a lesser road (with a wall on your right) and keep climbing. There are many fine trees in the cemetery and you may see squirrels.

On the left at the top of the rise is a monument to Highland Mary (Mary Campbell), who was betrothed to Robert Burns but died of typhus before they could marry. Her remains were moved here in 1920 (see also Walk 25, Dunoon). Also here is the James Watt cairn, erected in 1936 to mark the bicentenary of the birth of the great engineer, who was born in Greenock.

From here, take the next path on the left, turn right at the first junction, curve left, cross another junction, curve left again, meet the perimeter path by the wall and in about 80m leave the cemetery at a gate. Turn right.

Follow Bow Road uphill and continue all the way to the junction with Grieve Road. Turn right and continue climbing, with a wall on

WALK 19

81

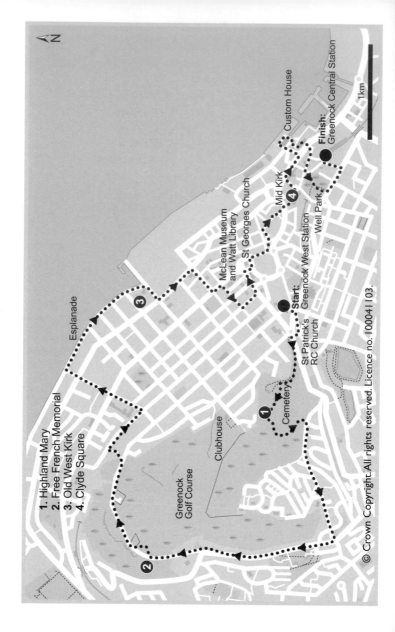

1. Highland Mary
2. Free French Memorial
3. Old West Kirk
4. Clyde Square

Esplanade

McLean Museum and Watt Library

St Georges Church

Mid Kirk

Custom House

Finish:
Greenock Central Station

Start:
Greenock West Station

St Patrick's RC Church

Cemetery

Well Park

Greenock Golf Course

Clubhouse

N

1km

© Crown Copyright. All rights reserved. Licence no. I0004 I 03.

your right. At a small roundabout, go straight ahead on Lyle Road. You can now see the striking Free French Monument ahead.

Walk up to the monument, which is in the form of an anchor. It honours "the memory of sailors of the Free French Forces who never ceased their fight for the liberation of France". Many of these brave men sailed from the Clyde between 1940 and 1945.

The monument commands a magnificent view across the Firth of Clyde taking in Dunoon and Hunter's Quay, the Gare Loch, Rhu and line upon line of hills. The harbour and Battery Park are far below. It is a place to linger.

When you are ready to leave, walk up towards the curious 'beacon' ahead (there is a view indicator here), cross the road and go up steps and then by a rough path to

The Free French monument.

the summit of Lyle Hill, from where the view extends further east to Helensburgh and back through Port Glasgow towards the city. The final part of the hill is rocky and needs a little care.

Go back to the path and turn right, with the golf course on your right. Walk down to the road, cross and continue downhill, enjoying the view ahead. Pass Windrush House and at the end of the grassy area look for steps on the left. Walk down the steps to Finnart Street and turn right. In 400 metres take the first left, Madeira Street, past Greenock Academy and follow the road all the way down to the Esplanade. Turn right for a bracing walk along by the Clyde. There are more good views – if you look carefully you can see Dumbarton Rock (Walk 17).

On the right just before the Clydeport Terminal is the old West Kirk, which has an interesting history. It started life as the North

WALK 19

83

Statue of Watt at the James Watt Memorial College.

Church in Nicholson Street in 1592. Much altered and extended, it lay empty for many years but in 1925 was moved to its present site, rebuilt and renovated.

Follow the road to the right and then turn left (Brougham Street). Take the second right (Patrick Street) up to Ardgowan Square, and turn left on Union Street. On the left is the Tontine Hotel. When built as an elegant house for Bailie Robertson in 1803, it marked the western edge of the town. Also on the left (no 1) is a fine mansion designed in Dutch Renaissance style by Sir Rowand Anderson in 1886. It was the estate office for the Shaw Stewart family and carries their coat of arms.

A little further along is the McLean Museum and Watt Library. The library dates from 1837, with the hall and museum added in 1876. Greenock's original library, marked by an inscription here, was the first public library in Scotland when it opened in 1783. The museum contains much of interest and has a cannon reputed to be from the Spanish Armada outside. The first Burns Club in Scotland was formed here in 1801.

Walk up Kelly Street, then turn left on Brisbane Street. Ahead now is the impressive St George's Church (1870), in the square of the same name, with the large Sheriff Court close by. Turn left past the church then right, down past the bus station. Go left (Kilblain Street), then right, down steps, through the underpass and walk all the way through the Oak Mall shopping centre, following signs to Clyde Square.

At the centre of the square is a powerful sculpture by Naomi Hunt called *Men of the Clyde*. Much of the square has been redeveloped, but there are pleasant small gardens and the Clydesdale Bank building of 1899 (James Thomson) has fine detail in its architecture.

Continue into Cathcart Square. Here you find the elegant Mid Kirk, built in 1761, though the 45m steeple was not completed until 20 years later. The portico was based on that of St Martin's-in-the-Fields in London. The square was chosen by Lord Cathcart, who owned the ground, to be the new centre of the town as it expanded in the latter part of the 18th century. Dominating the square is the Victoria Tower, which rises for 75m. Below it is an arched carriageway, and close by is an elegant Victorian fountain.

The tower forms part of the Municipal Buildings complex, a typically strong group of its

The clock tower on Custom House Quay, with the Waverley behind.

period with plenty of exterior decoration, making a statement to the outside world that Greenock was a thriving burgh.

Walk round the square and then down William Street, which once led to the main harbour area. On the left is the quaint Dutch Gable House. Built in 1755, it was restored in the 1980s. On the right is a doorway dated 1752, the oldest survivor of the 18th-century town. As you reach the dual carriageway, note on the corner the statue of James Watt.

Turn right, and in about 200m, cross the road at the lights. Walk down Brymner Street to Custom House Quay. Pass to the left of the splendid Custom House, built in 1818 to a design by William Burn and considered among the finest examples of its kind anywhere in Britain.

WALK 19

View over the Firth of Clyde.

Continue round the Custom House. The seafront has an expansive view across the Clyde to Helensburgh and a delicate cast iron clock tower from 1868. Continue around the square and walk across gardens past a large white anchor. Recross the road at the lights and turn right into Cathcart Street. This was once the business centre for the town, and notable buildings include the old General Post Office and the James Watt pub, which face each other across Cross Shore Street. Both are confident examples of Victorian architecture.

Go up steps on the left into Well Park. Keep climbing up to the top of the park from where there is a good view of the town. Walk past the large war memorial and exit at the main gate, turning left along Regent Street. Turn left on Terrace Road to the station.

PAISLEY

Distance	5km (3 miles) circular.
Start and Finish	Paisley Gilmour Street Station.
Underfoot	Pavement and surfaced paths.
Public transport	Frequent trains from Glasgow Central.
Refreshments	Good choice in the town centre.
Toilets	In the two shopping centres and in the Museum (when open).
Opening hours	Paisley Abbey Mon-Sat 10.00-15.30 (*www.paisleyabbey.org. uk*). Paisley Museum and Art Gallery Tue-Sat 10.00-17.00, Sun 14.00-17.00. Coats Observatory same hours as Museum. Sma' Shot Cottages Wed, Sat 12.00-16.00 Apr-Sept (*www.smashot.co.uk*). Coats Memorial Church, Fri 14.00-16.00 May-Sept.

Paisley folk, known as 'Buddies', are rightly proud of their town and its long history. This walk will show that there is much to see and admire.

From Gilmour Street Station, exit to Old Sneddon Street and turn left. Turn left under the railway, then right, along Hunter Street. At its end go steeply uphill to the left on a path into Oakshaw Street East. Turn right. The grey and white building, now part of Oakshaw Trinity Church hall, was from 1822 to 1889 a charity school founded by Margaret Hutcheson. Continue to the Coats Observatory, the first link with the textile industry that has been so important to Paisley. Thousands of people worked in the Coats and Clark thread-making factories. Both families were major civic benefactors, and the Observatory was a gift by Thomas Coats in 1882.

Return along Oakshaw Street East, and just before the former charity school, turn right into Orr Street, a narrow cobbled lane. Walk down to Wellmeadow Street and turn right.

On the right is Paisley's Museum and Art Gallery. Gifted by Sir Peter Coats in 1871, this was the first publicly-run museum in Scotland and holds a renowned collection of Paisley shawls. Next is the imposing Coats Memorial Church, built in memory of Thomas Coats. Designed by Hippolyte Blanc, it opened in 1894. The eight-arched crown is very fine and the church interior is rich with marble and alabaster.

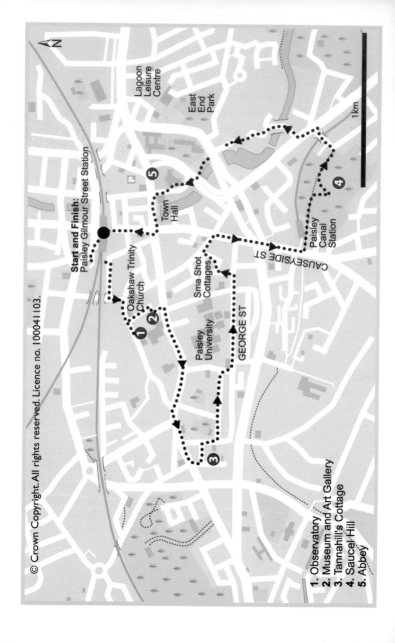

Start and Finish:
Paisley Gilmour Street Station

Oakshaw Trinity Church

Town Hall

Sma Shot Cottages

Paisley University

GEORGE ST

CAUSEYSIDE ST

Paisley Canal Station

Lagoon Leisure Centre

East End Park

1km

1. Observatory
2. Museum and Art Gallery
3. Tannahill's Cottage
4. Saucel Hill
5. Abbey

Note across the road the statue of John Witherspoon (1723-94) outside Paisley University. More of him later. Continue through Wellmeadow Street into Broomlands Street, cross and take the second left, Queen Street. Down here is Tannahill's Cottage. We have come from the mill owners to the humble house of a weaver. But Robert Tannahill, who lived here from 1775 until his untimely death in 1810, gained greater re-

Anchor Mill.

nown as a poet, and an inscription reads: "He sang amid the shuttles with the music of the woods".

From the cottage, walk along Cross Street, turn right into Castle Street, and first left into Argyle Street. At its end, turn right into Lady Lane, noting the fine decorated arch on the tenement opposite, and left into George Street. In 400 metres you pass the original entrance to the University, a grand classical building designed by a Paisley man, T.G.Abercrombie, in 1898 in the style of a Renaissance palazzo.

Turn left into George Place to see the Sma' Shot Cottages. These typical 18th-century weavers' dwellings are now run by the Old Paisley Society as a fascinating museum. The garden was created by the Groundforce team from *The Beechgrove Garden*. Continue into Shuttle Street and turn right into New Street. Opposite is Paisley Arts Centre. This was originally the Laigh Kirk, where John Witherspoon was minister. He was renowned for fierce attacks on drink and gambling, and also disliked the theatre, so he might not approve of the conversion! Witherspoon emigrated to America, became Principal of Princeton University and signed the Declaration of Independence in 1776.

Turn right at the lights into Causeyside. Note on the corner the Art Deco-style Russell Institute, gifted as a clinic by Miss Agnes Russell in 1927 in memory of her two brothers. Cross Gordon Street and continue, passing on the right the Laigh Kirk.

At Paisley Canal Station, turn left on the path (not the steps) and continue along the path and cycleway, right of the railway, into

Saucel Hill Park. As you do so, look left to see the Elipta, an unusual oval apartment block developed by the Cargill Group and opened in 2008.

It is worth climbing the grassy hill (no path) for a great view looking north over the town and motorway to the airport and the hills beyond. Leave the park and turn immediately left. Cross the railway and walk down to Lonend. Turn left. Cross at the lights, go left, then right, over the restored footbridge, and continue past the fine Anchor Mill, a listed building now superbly rejuvenated as high-class apartments.

Paisley Abbey.

Go through the blue gates at Anchor Business Centre and then go left on the riverside path. To the left is a good view of the rocks and weir with the White Cart living up to its name as it tumbles over. Continue with the path to Abbey Bridge, cross the road and go right to reach Paisley Abbey. This magnificent building dates back 900 years and is still in regular use. It contains so much of interest that it is worth spending plenty of time here to appreciate the architecture and serene atmosphere of the Abbey to the full. The Abbey replaced an older church dedicated to St Mirin, Paisley's patron saint, whose name lives on in the town's football team, St Mirren FC.

When you leave the Abbey, walk past the handsome Town Hall, paid for by the Clark family in the 1870s. Turn left on Gauze St and walk along to Dunn Square, an open space paid for by a Liberal MP, William Dunn, and designed by James Donald, a student of 'Greek' Thomson. Statues include two of Thomas and Peter Coats and one of Queen Victoria erected just after her death in 1901. One unusual aspect of the Coats' philanthropy was that, following an expedition which they funded, part of Antarctica was named Coats Land.

Cross the road at Paisley Cross and walk up past the powerful war memorial and across County Square to return to the station.

WALK 20

KILMARNOCK

Distance	4.5km (3.2 miles) circular.
Start and Finish	Kilmarnock Railway Station.
Underfoot	Pavement and good paths.
Public transport	Regular train service from Glasgow Central. There are also express buses from Glasgow Buchanan Street (X77) to Kilmarnock.
Refreshments	Selection of cafes and pubs in the town centre.
Toilets	In the Burns Mall.
Opening hours	The Dick Institute Museum is open Tue-Sat, 11.00-17.00, and is free. The Burns Monument Centre is open Mon-Thur, 9.15-16.45 and Fri, 9.15-15.45.

Kilmarnock has a long history and there is much of interest to see in the town. From the station, take the Town Centre exit, turn left, cross Garden Street and follow West George Street round and under the 23-arch viaduct, a superb piece of early railway engineering completed in 1850. Over to the right is the Square of Ales, named after Kilmarnock's twin town in southern France.

Go right, across the car park, to the Old High Kirk, opened in 1734 (the steeple was added six years later). Go round the church to the graveyard behind to find a memorial to John Wilson, who printed the Kilmarnock Edition of Burns' poems. Exit to Soulis Street. Set into the wall to the right is the Soulis Monument, a replica cross of 1825.

Turn left, cross the road at the junction with care, and walk up High Street. Cross the Kilmarnock Water and immediately turn right into Kay Park. Fork left, climbing. Go up steps onto the main path. On the left is the Reformers' Monument, erected in 1885 to mark 'Kilmarnock Pioneers of Parliamentary Reform' from the early 18th century.

Walk back along the main path to the Burns Monument (1879), which is the centrepiece of a study and research centre for local and family history opened in 2009. The monument, featuring a statue of Burns by W.G. Stevenson, cost £10,000, a huge sum for the time, and was the gift of Alexander Kay, a local businessman who also donated the park to the town. To its left is a handsome fountain, erected in 1902 to mark the coronation of King Edward VII.

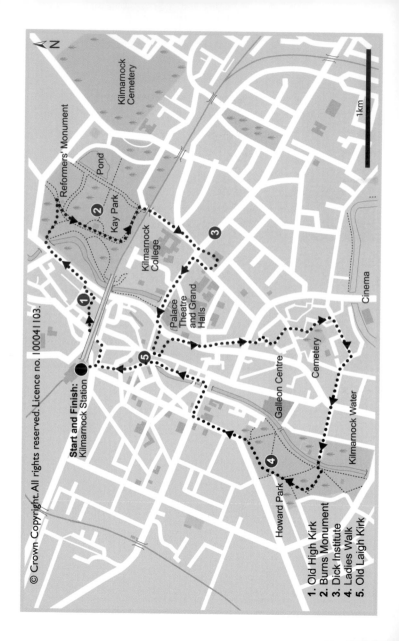

N

Start and Finish:
Kilmarnock Station

Reformers' Monument

Pond

Kay Park

Kilmarnock Cemetery

Kilmarnock College

Palace Theatre and Grand Halls

Galleon Centre

Cemetery

Kilmarnock Water

Howard Park

Cinema

1. Old High Kirk
2. Burns Monument
3. Dick Institute
4. Ladies Walk
5. Old Laigh Kirk

1km

The Old High Kirk.

Continue with the main path, swinging left to exit the park through gates. You may see squirrels scampering up the trees. Turn right, under the railway, and continue past Kilmarnock College.

Cross London Road at the lights and walk left to the Dick Institute (public library and museum). The building, gifted by James Dick, was opened in 1901 and is crowned by a statue of Minerva, Roman goddess of wisdom and art.

Leave by the main gates, noting the imposing War Memorial opposite, turn right, walk back to London Road and turn left, passing a statue of James Dick and then the 1927 Masonic Temple, home to four lodges. Follow the road down to the river, passing on the right the Henderson Church, opened in 1907 and named for Alexander Henderson, joint author of the National Covenant.

Statue of Burns and Wilson at The Cross.

Cross the river. On the left is the Palace Theatre and Grand Halls complex. This was designed by James Ingram in 1862 as a Corn Exchange, with the theatre (still in regular use) added in 1903.

Use the underpass and walk through Burns Mall to The Cross, with its central statue of Burns and Wilson, unveiled by the Princess Royal in 1996. The printworks where John Wilson produced Burns' poems was in this area. Turn left on King Street, take the first lane on the left, cross the car park and turn right down Sturrock Street. Cross at the lights and continue down on a path through trees.

At the next junction, cross and take the path left of the Baptist Church. Go right, past garages, then left on Gallion Walk. Cross the next road, heading slightly right onto Newton Walk (there are two of these, so don't be confused!). Follow the path to the high wall, which surrounds an old graveyard where Johnnie Walker, who founded the famous whisky company, was buried.

Follow the wall left, then take the road out to Lawson Street and turn right. Swing round to the right (noting the wall plaque to John-nie Walker) and cross into East, then West, Netherton Street. Cross the footbridge leading into Howard Park. Go left, then right (cycle-path signs), join the main path and turn right at the monument to Alexander Marshall MD, a doctor here for 42 years. You are now on the Lady's Walk, named for an 18th-century Countess of Kilmarnock, who often walked here from her home at Kilmarnock House while waiting for news of her husband, a Jacobite sympathiser who had been captured. Sadly for her, he was executed at Tower Hill in London in August 1746. Fork right, still inside the park, and leave at the main gates.

Walks up Dundonald Road, with the Congregational Church on the left and the Sheriff Court on the right. At the crossroads, note Holy Trinity Church to the left. It has a fine chancel designed by Sir Giles Gilbert Scott. John Finnie Street (ahead) is considered one of the finest examples of Victorian street planning in Scotland. It is named after the man who largely paid for its construction. The original buildings included a grand Opera House.

Turn right on St Marnock Street (named for the town's patron saint), past the old Sheriff Court of 1852 (near the site of Kilmarnock House). Across the road is St Marnock's Church. On the wall of the Old Sheriff Court, easily missed, is a plaque commemorating the Kilmarnock and Troon Railway, the first in Scotland, opened by the Duke of Portland in 1812 with horse-drawn trucks carrying coal. Steam was introduced as early as 1817.

Cross the Kilmarnock Water and then go left along Sandbed Street. This was once one of the town's most important thoroughfares. Follow it up to the Old Laigh Kirk.

Old Laigh Kirk.

The earliest parts of the building date back to the 16th century, but most of it was constructed in 1802, after 29 people were killed when part of the earlier church collapsed. The church has superb stained glass windows. Outside is a rather gruesome memorial holding the heads (only) of John Ross and John Shields, who were executed in Edinburgh in 1766 for their religious beliefs.

There is a statue of Johnnie Walker outside the Kirk. From the statue, take the right fork up Strand Street. In this area was the headquarters of Walkers, whose whisky has become world-famous with its slogan "Born in 1820, still going strong".

Go up the steps, cross the road and turn left for the station, parts of which date from 1877 (the line itself opened as early as 1843).

WALK 21

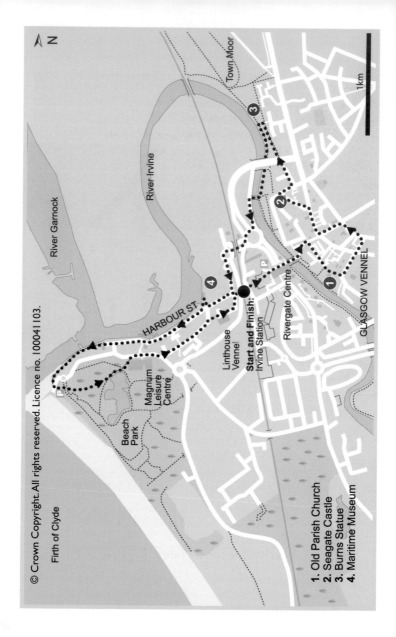

N

Firth of Clyde

River Garnock

River Irvine

Town Moor

HARBOUR ST

Start and Finish:
Irvine Station

Linthouse Vennel

Rivergate Centre

GLASGOW VENNEL

Beach Park

Magnum Leisure Centre

1. Old Parish Church
2. Seagate Castle
3. Burns Statue
4. Maritime Museum

1km

IRVINE

Distance	5km (3 miles) circular.
Start and Finish	Irvine Station.
Underfoot	Pavement and good paths.
Public transport	Regular train service from Glasgow Central.
Refreshments	Selection of cafes and pubs in the town centre. Café at the Maritime Museum.
Toilets	In the Rivergate Centre and at Low Green and the sea front.
Opening hours	The Scottish Maritime Museum is open daily, 10.00-17.00. The Heckling Shed can be visited Friday and Saturday, 10.00-13.00 and 14.00-17.00.

Although Irvine is one of our New Towns, it has been a Royal Burgh since 1372 and has plenty of historical and scenic interest.

Leave the station by the main exit, cross the road at the lights and walk up to the Rivergate Centre. Go in, up the escalator and follow the malls round to the left. The Centre was built on the site of the old bridge over the River Irvine, a crossing since 1533.

Exit the centre into Bridgegate. On the right is the Trinity Community Centre, an excellent example of positive re-use of an old church. Turn right up Hill Street (at Irvine Buttery) and climb this very attractive lane. Cross into Peden Place and continue to the Old Parish Church. Built in 1772 to a design by David Muir, it has superb stained glass including a beautiful 'Tree of Life' window designed by Susan Bradbury and installed in 1996 to mark the bicentenary of Robert Burns' death. Burns was a regular worshipper here while living in Irvine in 1781-83.

Go round the side of the church and exit to Kirk Vennel. Turn left. Cross Townhead and continue into Glasgow Vennel, another lovely old street, with several Burns links. The poet lodged at no 4 for a time and at no 10 is the heckling shed where he worked, now an art gallery ('heckling' originally meant to comb out yarn).

Turn left (Cotton Row), left on the path to East Road and left again down to the High Street. Turn right, passing the fine Town House of 1859, topped by an octagonal clock tower. On the pavement outside

Old houses in Hill Street.

the Eglinton Arms is a roundel showing the plants used by Dr Fleming to treat Burns in November 1781 when "luckless fortune's northern storms laid a' my blossoms low".

Turn left into Seagate, an old cobbled lane. On the right is the ruin of Seagate Castle, actually a grand town house built for the Montgomeries, Earls of Eglinton, in 1562-85 but abandoned in the 1740s. Mary Queen of Scots stayed here as a guest of the Earl when it was a new building, accompanied by her attendants known as the 'Four Maries'.

From Seagate, turn right, then first left (Academy Street, not named). Cross the footbridge over the ring road and continue on the path to the statue of Burns. It was moved here in 1996 to mark his bicentenary. Beyond him is the Town Moor.

Turn back here and follow the riverside path, a pleasant walk beside the Irvine. Go under the road and continue to the footbridge, with Low Green ahead.

Cross the river and turn left along Waterside. Go right at the roundabout, cross two roads, turn left, go right past Fullarton Church (due to be demolished as this book was written) and pass under the railway to Victoria Roundabout. All this area was once a separate township called Fullarton.

Go round the roundabout anti-clockwise, and once past The Moorings, a new housing development, turn into Cochrane Street. At its end, turn right into Montgomery Street. The steep gables on the end houses led to them being affectionately known locally as 'the Bookends'. On the right, opposite Gottries Road, is the Scottish Maritime Museum, founded in 1983 and containing many items of interest, including old ships being restored.

Continue down Harbour Street, passing further sections of the Maritime Museum. No 132 was at one time the Custom House. There

The jetty at the sea front.

is a broad view looking north across the river. The fine statue, *The Carter and his Horse* by David Annand, marks the fact that in the mid-18th century, Irvine was the second most important port in Scotland and coal was a major trading commodity.

Pass the Ship Inn, which has been a hostelry since 1754. The bridge on the right with inscribed names of famous engineers such as Watt and Telford led over to The Big Idea, a science museum now closed.

Continue to the jetty at the sea front. To the left, a glorious sandy beach stretches away south. This is a popular walk leading in 11km to Troon, which you can see on the horizon. Cross the car park and take the tarmac path from it leading across to an attractive pond which usually holds good birdlife.

Keep left of the pond and take the path past the Magnum Leisure Centre. Cross the road and turn left into Gottries Road. Continue ahead past two fine classical buildings, one of them with an intriguing 'abstract' metal ship outside, into Linthouse Vennel, named for the huge engine shed here, which was originally sited at Linthouse Yard in Govan. Turn left into the Vennel, noting the beautifully restored houses, and right into Montgomerie Street to return to the station.

WALK 22

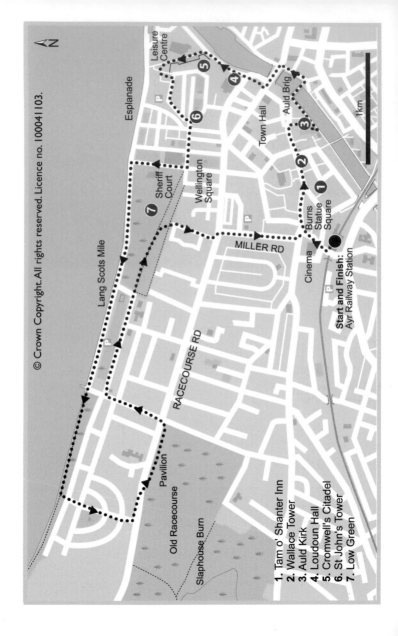

N

Esplanade

Leisure
Centre

Town Hall

Auld Brig

Sheriff Court

Wellington Square

Lang Scots Mile

Burns Statue Square

MILLER RD

Cinema

RACECOURSE RD

Pavilion

Old Racecourse

Slaphouse Burn

1km

Start and Finish:
Ayr Railway Station

1. Tam o' Shanter Inn
2. Wallace Tower
3. Auld Kirk
4. Loudoun Hall
5. Cromwell's Citadel
6. St John's Tower
7. Low Green

AYR

Distance	6km (4 miles) circular.
Start and Finish	Ayr Railway Station (or nearby car park).
Underfoot	Pavement and surfaced paths.
Public transport	Regular trains from Glasgow Central. There are also express buses (X77) from Buchanan Street bus station, and (X16) from Hamilton and East Kilbride.
Refreshments	Wide choice in town centre.
Toilets	At the station, town centre and Pavilion.

This walk explores the historic heart of Ayr and also provides a good helping of bracing sea air. Ayrshire is Burns country, and from the station you enter Burns Statue Square, with the poet (by George Lawson) gazing south towards Alloway. When the statue was unveiled in July 1891, the crowd was estimated at 40,000 people.

Keep to the right, round into Alloway Street, to reach the Tam o' Shanter Inn. It dates back over 250 years, and naturally, Burns is said to have enjoyed his share of revelry here, as did Douglas Graham of Shanter, on whom Tam's character was based.

Now step further back in time with the Wallace Tower, designed by Thomas Hamilton in 1832. The great patriot warrior is said to have been imprisoned in an earlier tower here. Continue along High Street to Kirk Port, a small lane, and turn right under the 17th-century lychgate to reach the beautiful Auld Kirk of 1654, built here after Cromwell's troops occupied the previous church on the sands. The church is dedicated to St John the Baptist and is still used for worship.

Walk down to the River Ayr and turn briefly right to see a stone commemorating a number of Covenanting martyrs. Turn back and walk along to the Auld Brig, started in the 13th century. Cross the river. There are usually swans and ducks on the water. At the far side, turn left to Ayr Bridge: opposite is the Black Bull, originally a coaching inn called Simpsons and mentioned by Burns in 1786. At the foot of the bridge is the old mercat cross of Newton-upon-Ayr.

Recross the river and turn right at the lights (Boat Vennel). Ahead is the fine 1825 Town Hall with its 68-metre steeple, a landmark for miles around. It is by the same architect as the Wallace Tower.

The Auld Brig.

Walk down to Loudoun Hall. This is the oldest house in Ayr, built around 1513 as a semi-fortified town house for James Tait, a wealthy trader. It was later home to the hereditary sheriff of Ayr, the Earl of Loudoun, hence the name. Mary, Queen of Scots stayed here (almost inevitably?) in August 1563. The building has been restored, and is now a cultural centre for the town.

Continue along South Harbour Street. On the left in Fort Street is Ayr Academy. The three stone heads of Robert Burns, Sir David Wilkie and James Watt represent literature, art and science.

Reach the walls of Cromwell's Citadel. Finished in 1654, it was the largest of the five forts he had built in Scotland. It housed over 1,200 troops, but on Cromwell's death in 1660 its military use ceased. Turn left by the walls and walk along the path towards the sea. Take the first path on the left and the first left again.

Turn right into Arran Terrace, continue along Ailsa Place (more fort wall here shows how extensive it was) and at the junction look left to see St John's Tower, all that remains of the 13th-century Kirk of St John the Baptist. The Scottish Parliament met here in 1315 to settle the succession of Robert the Bruce.

Turn right along Cassilis Street and continue to Wellington Square, a pleasant open space with statues facing the imposing County Buildings (now the Sheriff Court). There is also a memorial to John

Loudon MacAdam, the pioneer road-builder, who was born in Ayr (in the building in Sandgate currently housing the Tourist Information Centre) in 1756.

Turn right into Pavilion Road. On the left is Low Green, a large open space (18ha) given to the new Royal Burgh by King William the Lion in 1205 and maintained for public use ever since. This may well be Scotland's oldest public open space. Walk along to the Esplanade and turn left. Step out beside the sea with the fresh air filling your lungs. You are on the 'Lang Scots Mile', a popular local walk marking the fact that in the past, a Scots mile was 1984 yards, whereas

St John's Tower.

the 'English mile' was 1760 yards. There is a great view looking south to the Heads of Ayr and across the water to Arran.

You can shorten the walk by turning left at the end of Low Green. For the full walk continue as below.

Carry on past Low Green. In the middle distance you may see Greenan Castle, a ruined Kennedy stronghold. Continue past a beach restaurant, and in about another 500 metres, take the first surfaced path on the left into Carwinshoch View. At its end, turn left on the main road.

Just past Nightingale House, cross the road and turn left along the path inside the wall to the Old Racecourse Pavilion. This was indeed the site of Ayr Racecourse before it moved to its present location north of the river. It is now playing fields and a golf course.

Continue with the path, and at the lights, cross and walk down Seafield Road. At the roundabout turn right into Blackburn Drive, and back at Low Green (the short walk rejoins here) take the path straight ahead. About two-thirds of the way up the green go right, across the grass past seats, then through a gap in the wall and into Fairfield Road.

Cross into Miller Road and walk back to Burns Statue Square and the station.

WALK 23

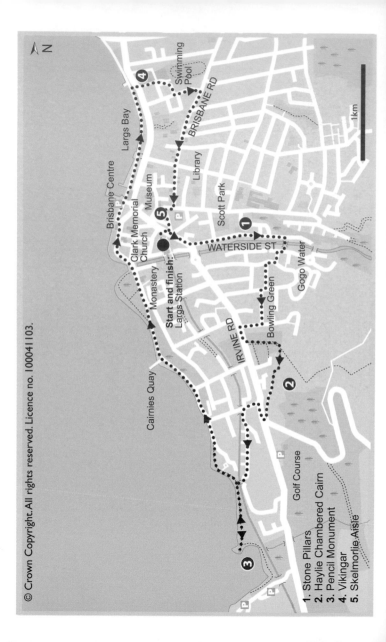

N

Swimming Pool

BRISBANE RD

Largs Bay

Brisbane Centre

Library

Clark Memorial Church

Museum

Scott Park

Monastery

Start and finish: Largs Station

WATERSIDE ST

Gogo Water

Cairnies Quay

IRVINE RD

Bowling Green

Golf Course

1 km

1. Stone Pillars
2. Haylie Chambered Cairn
3. Pencil Monument
4. Vikingar
5. Skelmorlie Aisle

LARGS

Distance	5km (3 miles) circular.
Start and Finish	Largs Station.
Underfoot	Pavement and good paths. The steps up to the stone pillars are slippery and overgrown.
Public transport	Regular train service, or Citylink bus 906, from Glasgow.
Refreshments	Selection of cafes and pubs in the town. Café at Vikingar.
Toilets	At the pier and at Vikingar (if open).
Opening hours	Vikingar is open daily 10.30-17.30 Apr-Sept; daily 10.30-15.30 Oct and Mar; weekends only 10.30-15.30 Nov and Feb; closed Dec-Jan. Largs Museum is open Mon-Sat 14.00-17.00.

Largs is still a popular resort, but most visitors stay around the pier area, or take the ferry to Cumbrae. Venture a little further, and you will find there is much to see and enjoy.

From the station, turn right, out to Main Street, and cross the busy road at the lights. Turn right and then third left into Waterside Street. On the left, just after the Red Cross building, is Green Hill, which is topped by three curious stone pillars. These were erected in 1808 as an observatory by Sir Thomas Brisbane. Born in Largs in 1773, he was a career soldier who was appointed Governor of New South Wales in 1821, although the city named after him is in Queensland. He was also a noted astronomer. He is remembered each summer in Largs by a Brisbane Queen Festival. To the left, overgrown, slippery wooden steps lead up to the pillars, but they can be made out from below.

Continue up Waterside Street. Just after no 74, turn right on a path that leads to a footbridge over the Gogo Water. Once across, turn right and left three times in quick succession and then right down Bankhouse Avenue to Irvine Road. Turn left and then left again into Douglas Park. Walk round the bowling green, admiring the formal garden to the left, and at the main path turn left (sign to Haylie Chambered Cairn).

Follow the path uphill and right and continue on a grassy path behind houses. Just through a gate, on the left is the cairn. When discovered in 1772 by James Wilson of Haylie, it still contained the remains of five people. The tomb is at least 5,000 years old and it is amazing that it has survived all that time.

Continue down the path, now flagged, and walk past Haylie House (an old people's home) and down its drive with good views across to Cumbrae. You will probably see the ferries shuttling back and forth on the short trip across to the island.

Cross the main road at the lights and turn right, then first left (Anthony Road). Take the first left (Walkerston Avenue) and at its end go over the railway on the footbridge and turn left on the shore path. This path was remade 100 years ago as a project for the unemployed, largely funded by public subscription.

The Pencil Monument.

Follow the path along the shore to the tall Pencil Monument, which commemorates the naval Battle of Largs in 1263. King Alexander III defeated Haakon of Norway, thus starting the long withdrawal of Norse power in western and northern Scotland – a decisive moment in Scottish history. Beyond the monument is Largs Yacht Haven, a large marina.

Turn here and enjoy the walk back all the way along the Promenade towards the town centre. Shore plants include flag irises and thrift, and there are good views to Cumbrae and northwards along the front. At the grass area on the right (known as The Broomfields) is a small jetty called Cairnies Quay. This was built by a Dr Cairnie who moored a yacht here in the 19th century. He created the first ever man-made curling pond in the grounds of his home, called Curling Hall, and he is recognised as one of the true pioneers of the sport.

Continue along the Promenade past a large adventure play area. On the right is a house unusually used as a Benedictine Monastery. Cross the Makdougall Brisbane Bridge over the Gogo Water, also named for Sir Thomas. To the right is the Clark Memorial Church

(1890), with its tall spire. It has a fine hammerbeam roof, and good contemporary stained glass.

Pass the Brisbane Centre (formerly the town baths). Reach the pier, always a busy place, and continue northwards, passing – not named for me and designed for kids a bit younger than myself – Jolly Roger's Adventureland!

Walk on, enjoying the sea views. On the right is Our Lady Star of the Sea, the Catholic Church built in 1962 with a notable Madonna by Hew Lorimer.

At the putting green, go right to Vikingar, the centre that tells the story of the Norsemen (5-screen a/v presentation, and Viking Hall of Knowledge). Opened in 1995, the complex incorporates the Barrfield Theatre, opened in 1930 with funds donated by local benefactor Robert Barr and still in regular use today.

Leaving the centre, turn left twice and then right on Brisbane Road. Cross Nelson Street into Boyd Street. At its end, go right on Gateside Street to find (across the road ahead) the Skelmorlie Aisle. This should not be missed. It is a 17th-century gem with painted timber ceiling and canopied tomb to the Montgomerie family. Alongside is the smaller Brisbane Aisle.

The key to the Aisle can be obtained from Largs Museum, round the corner and also worth a visit. After leaving the Aisle or the Museum it is a short step back to the station.

The seashore at Largs.

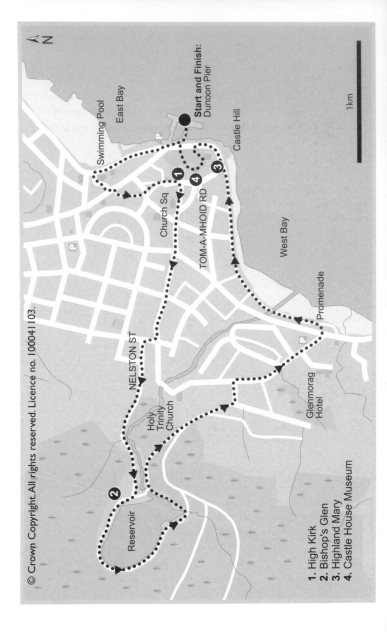

© Crown Copyright. All rights reserved. Licence no. 100041103.

N

Swimming Pool

East Bay

Start and Finish:
Dunoon Pier

Castle Hill

Church Sq

TOM-A-MHOID RD

West Bay

NELSTON ST

Promenade

Holy Trinity Church

Glenmorag Hotel

Reservoir

Castle House Museum

1km

1. High Kirk
2. Bishop's Glen
3. Highland Mary
4. Castle House Museum

Distance	5.5km (3.5 miles) circular.
Start and Finish	Dunoon Pier.
Underfoot	Pavement and good paths. No special footwear needed.
Public transport	Excellent integrated hourly train/ferry from Glasgow Central via Gourock.
Refreshments	Good choice in Dunoon.
Toilets	At the swimming pool and at West Bay.
Opening hours	Castle House Museum: Easter-Oct, Mon-Sat 10.30-16.30, Sun 14.00-16.30. Admission charge (children free). The High Kirk is usually open May-Sept, Mon-Fri 10.00-16.00.

It is always a pleasure to go 'doon the watter' for a day in Dunoon, where there is much to see. As well as the town itself, this walk takes in a local beauty spot.

After the enjoyable 25-minute sail from Gourock, leave the pier and turn right. Across the road is the fine Cenotaph war memorial. Continue along the front, passing the Tourist Information Centre and the swimming pool (public toilets). Turn left into Moir Street.

Cross Argyll Street and turn left, noting the ornamental railings. Take the first pathway on the right, into a car park. Follow its exit road steeply uphill. Take Ferry Brae (an evocative name) and the first right, Kirk Street, to reach the High Kirk. There has been a church here for over 700 years, and it has borne various names. Until the late 17th century, Dunoon's church was a Cathedral of the Bishops of Argyll. The present building dates from 1817 (enlarged in 1839) and has a fine interior featuring a beautiful chancel window.

The clock dates from 1840, at which time the tower was heightened by 3m to accommodate it. It is one of the few 'gravity clocks' remaining. One oddity is that the south face of the clock is dark (the other faces are white), apparently to avoid confusing mariners.

Continue downhill and, at the bollards, turn right into Castle Street. On the right, a row of old cottages has been renovated by Cowal Camera Club as a clubroom. Also here is the site of the former Bishop's Palace.

Continue uphill along Tom-a-Mhoid Road, Wellington Street and then take a right fork into Auchamore Road. There are fine detached houses here, and the views across the Firth of Clyde steadily expand as you climb. Turn right on Alexander Street and first left on Nelson Street, passing a former farm on the left.

Near the end of the road, a small gallery on the left has a wall plaque which says 'in all things of nature there is something of the marvellous'. Continue on the narrow road into Bishop's Glen, with the Balgaidh Burn below to the left. This area was developed in the 1870s with the construction of three reservoirs to supply the town's water needs. These went out of commission in the 1970s and the area (known as Bishop's Glen only since the 1950s) is now used for recreation and forestry.

Before long you see the water cascading down the spillway of the one remaining reservoir, and then reach its banks at a small parking area for the disabled, with picnic tables. It is a very attractive scene with forestry climbing the hills and reflecting on the water. You will probably see fishermen trying their luck – the reservoir is stocked with trout.

Bishop's Glen.

Continue on the path round the reservoir. At the far end there is a small beach and more picnic tables. Fork left here to cross the burn on a footbridge. Continue along by the water, climbing a flight of steps and then passing through an area of tall old pines. At the next burn the path bends sharply left. Reach the spillway and drop down beside it.

At the next path fork, keep right (good views here) and walk out to the road. The old Holy Trinity Church on a hilltop site can be seen to the left. Keep left at a fork, on a rough road, then turn left and then right on Kilbride Road. Follow this road all the way down to the promenade and turn left to walk along West Bay, a bracing walk by the sea with wide views across the estuary. Hotels on the left have lovely gardens.

Above you in Tom-a-Mhoid Road is a memorial to 200 members of the Clan Lamont killed by Campbells in a brutal massacre in 1646. However, there are two sides to every story, and the Lamonts themselves

The Pier, Dunoon.

were hardly blameless in their conduct prior to the massacre. Tom-a-Mhoid means 'Moot Hill', and indicates a place where justicial decisions were proclaimed.

Keep going along the promenade, pass a roundabout where the road bends left, and then take a stepped path on the left to reach the statue to Highland Mary. Born in Dunoon in 1764, Mary Campbell was betrothed to Robert Burns, but died of typhus before the marriage could take place. Mary is buried in Greenock – see Walk 19. She gazes wistfully across the water towards Ayrshire, perhaps faintly hearing the beautiful songs that Burns wrote in her memory.

Continue to the top of the hill. There is a superb view across the Firth of Clyde, with an indicator pointing out all the landmarks.

Continue past the flagpole and down the steps to reach the Castle House Museum. This veritable treasure trove is well worth the small admission charge. Leave the museum, walk down the steps and across the road to the pier. In the garden is a memorial to Pipe Major John McLellan, a famed composer.

The pier (and roadway) were built in 1898 and the sea traffic was much busier in earlier days. Going 'doon the watter' to Dunoon is a classic journey for Glaswegians. The boats are as efficient as ever, but one sign of the times (literally) is that, most prominent on the sides of the ships, is the CalMac website name.

Dunoon's Victorian developers would have hoped to see travellers still visiting their town in the 21st century, but could never have foreseen that!

WALK 25

111

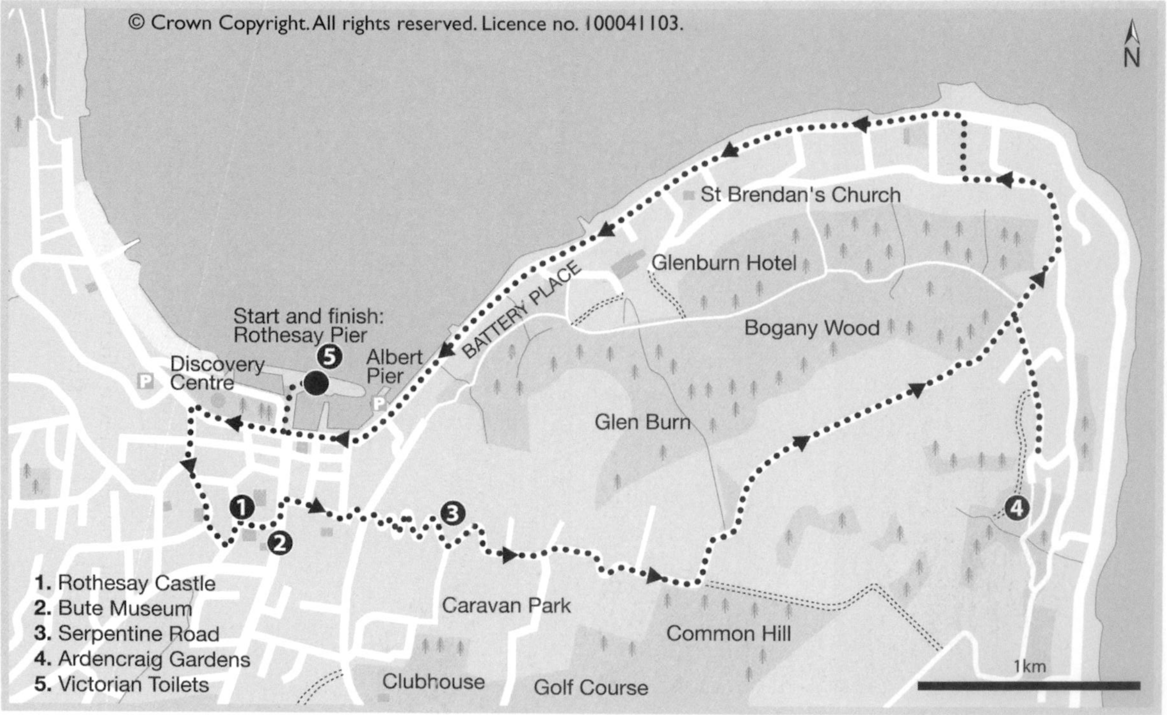
© Crown Copyright. All rights reserved. Licence no. 100041103.
N
St Brendan's Church
Glenburn Hotel
BATTERY PLACE
Bogany Wood
Start and finish:
Rothesay Pier
5
Albert
Pier
Discovery
Centre
P
Glen Burn
1
3
2
4
Caravan Park
Common Hill
Clubhouse
Golf Course
1km
1. Rothesay Castle
2. Bute Museum
3. Serpentine Road
4. Ardencraig Gardens
5. Victorian Toilets

ROTHESAY

Distance	5.5km (3.5 miles) circular.
Start and Finish	Rothesay Pier.
Underfoot	Pavement and quiet roads. One long, steep climb.
Public transport	Regular train and linking ferry service from Glasgow Central via Wemyss Bay.
Refreshments	Wide choice in the town. Restaurant/tearoom at Craigmore Pier.
Toilets	At Rothesay Pier.
Opening hours	Rothesay Castle: daily 09.30-18.30. Bute Museum: Mon-Sat 10.30-16.30, Sun 14.30-16.30. Ardencraig Gardens are open daily, May-Sept.
Further information	The island website at *www.isle-of-bute.com* will tell you more, and you can pick up good descriptive leaflets at the Discovery Centre.
Note	Parking at Wemyss Bay ferry terminal is very limited and it is recommended that you use the train to get there.

The enjoyable ferry trip to the island of Bute can be combined with a walk which delves into Rothesay's intriguing history and provides wonderful views.

From the pier, turn right and take the path through the attractive park past the former Winter Gardens, now the Isle of Bute Discovery Centre. Note the memorial stone to 300 Butemen who died at the Battle of Falkirk in 1298. Cross the road here and walk up Gallowgate, once indeed the start of a path leading to a point where criminals were hanged. Pass Montague Street (named for the wife of the 3rd Earl of Bute) and turn left on Ladeside, the name indicating that the small burn once powered mills.

Turn left along John Street, which has a fine row of original weavers' cottages with an 1805 datestone. Turn left down Mill Street to Rothesay Castle, a Stuart stronghold for over 500 years. Its almost circular design is unique in Scotland. It has a proper moat with ducks and large fish in it, and you can even hire the banqueting hall for functions.

Behind the castle is Bute Museum, worth a visit for the displays of local history and wildlife. From the Museum, walk out to High Street, noting the replica Mercat Cross, and opposite, the late 17th-

Rothesay.

century Mansion House, built for George Cunningham, an Edinburgh lawyer.

Walk up Castle Street, passing the solid, castellated Town Buildings, and where the road bends left, start up the sharp curves of the Serpentine Road. Take the steep path on the left until it runs out and then follow the road – a real test for motorists coming down!

Continue climbing, passing many fine villas. Rothesay expanded greatly in the 19th century once the railway reached Wemyss Bay, and well-to-do Glasgow families built houses here. Eastfield has fine carved stone lions and eagles.

Eventually the road levels out. At the high point there is a magnificent view of Rothesay, Loch Striven and the Kyles of Bute. Toward Castle is also prominent. Down below to the left is Skipper Wood and on the right a golf course.

Start downhill, now on Eastlands Road. Turn right on Ardencraig Lane. At its end a gate in the wall on the right leads into Ardencraig Gardens. This is truly a hidden gem, a glorious walled garden with formal beds, greenhouses full of beautiful plants, a small burn with water lilies and an aviary. Don't miss it. The gardens are 100 years old, and were originally the walled garden of a large estate. Some 50,000 plants are grown here each year for use both at Ardencraig and elsewhere on the island.

Return to Eastlands Road and continue downhill, swinging left into Crichton Road. At a stone wall on the right (opposite no 50) go right, down to the shore, and then left. Note the original names for some of the villas on the left, carved on the gateposts. Many have royal connections, including Royal Terrace itself. This followed a visit to Bute by Prince Leopold, son of Queen Victoria, in 1873.

Pass St Brendan's Church (rebuilt, but with the original tower retained). Bute folk are sometimes called Brendanes after the saint. Up on the left, the Glenburn Hotel was originally a Hydropathic Establishment where people came for water treatment believed to have healing properties.

Beattie Court, on the left, started life as Scotland's first Aquarium (opened by Prince Leopold), was then a public baths and a dance hall, and is now apart-

Looking over the Kyles of Bute.

ments. Note the fine lamp-posts. The originals were made by the Saracen Foundry in Glasgow in the 1870s, and were replaced to the same design in 1996.

This part of the road is called Battery Place, so named because guns were sited here at the time when it was feared that Napoleon might attack Britain (yes, even this far north). Opposite the outer harbour, the imposing building, now flats, was previously a public hall and later a cinema.

Return to the pier, still a focus for the town and recently greatly enlarged and redeveloped to take larger ferries. The elegant original 1882 buildings were largely destroyed by fire in 1962. However, there is one survival here that you should visit before you leave – Rothesay's famous Victorian Toilets. They date from 1899, and all the fireclay porcelain was made by Twyford's in Hanley, near Stoke-on-Trent, at an original cost of just £530.

Only the men's area is original, as ladies were not catered for a century ago – a discrimination which must have led to some anxious moments! The toilets were fully restored and a ladies' section added in 1994, giving both convenience and equality.

WALK 26

115

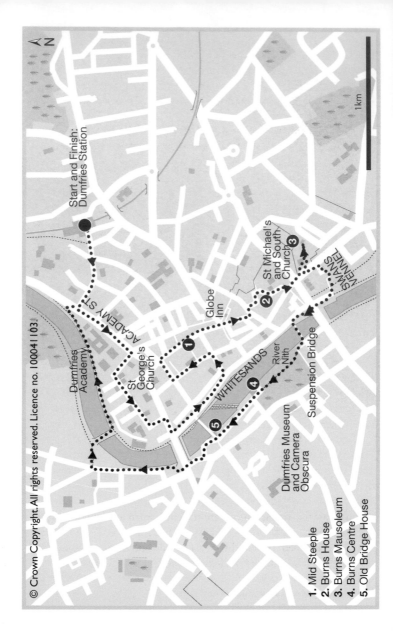

N

Start and Finish:
Dumfries Station

Dumfries Academy

ACADEMY ST

St George's Church

Globe Inn

St Michael's and South Church

1. Mid Steeple
2. Burns House
3. Burns Mausoleum
4. Burns Centre
5. Old Bridge House

1

2

3

4

5

VENNEL

SWANS

WHITESANDS

River Nith

Suspension Bridge

Dumfries Museum and Camera Obscura

Old Bridge House

1km

Distance	4km (2.5 miles) circular.
Start and Finish	Dumfries Station (or park at Whitesands and start the walk from there).
Underfoot	All pavement or good paths.
Public transport	Regular train service from Glasgow Central to Dumfries.
Refreshments	Good choice in town centre.
Toilets	At Whitesands.
Opening hours	Burns House, Old Bridge House: Apr-Sep Mon-Sat 10.00-17.00, Sun 14.00-17.00. Robert Burns Centre: Apr-Sep Mon-Sat 10.00-20.00, Sun 14.00-17.00, Oct-Mar Tue-Sat 10.00-13.00, Sun 14.00-17.00. All these are free. Dumfries Museum & Camera Obscura: Apr-Sep Mon-Sat 10.00-17.00, Sun 14.00-17.00, Oct-Mar Tue-Sat 10.00-13.00, 14.00-17.00. Museum free, charge for Camera Obscura. St Michael's Church: Apr-Sep Mon-Fri 10.00-16.00.
Further information	Burns Trail leaflet, free from the Tourist Information Centre at Whitesands.

Dumfries is noted for its Robert Burns associations, as will become clear on this pleasant stroll around the town, but there is much else to see and enjoy.

From the station, follow Lovers' Walk out to Academy Street and turn left, passing Dumfries Academy. The original baroque building in red sandstone (1897, F.J.Carruthers) is very striking. Turn right into Irving Street and then left along George Street. This was Dumfries's 'New Town', planned by architect Robert Burn (not Burns!) in 1806 and with many handsome buildings remaining. St George's Church dates from 1844. Turn left on Charlotte Street, right on Buccleuch Street for a short distance, and then left on Whitesands, once a market area (start here if you came by car).

Just past the Tourist Information Centre, turn left up Bank Street. Above the Burns Café are the rooms where Burns lived from 1791-93. Here he composed 'Ae Fond Kiss', 'Lea Rig' and many other wonderful songs; little wonder it is called the 'Sanghoose o' Scotland'.

Take the first left (Irish Street). There are a number of 18th-century buildings here, of which no 29 is perhaps the best. Turn right into

Statue of Burns and his dog Luath.

Friars Vennel. This was originally a route down to a ford across the river, and there were orchards here.

At the top of the brae is the 1882 marble statue of Burns, designed by Amelia Hill and carved in Italy. The representation of Burns' collie Luath is somewhat peculiar! Behind the statue is the almost incredibly ornate Greyfriars Church (1868, John Starforth).

Turn right along High Street, for centuries the heart of the town. Pass the Hole in the Wa' inn (1620) and reach Queensberry Square, with a tall obelisk (designed by Robert Adam in 1780) commemorating the Duke of Queensberry. Behind it is the handsome 1804 Trades Hall.

Also here is the Mid Steeple of 1707, on the site of the old Mercat Cross. Burns' body lay in state here before his funeral in July 1796. As he was being buried, his wife was giving birth to their son Michael. Wall plaques mark Dumfries's twinning with towns in Europe and the USA.

Pass an elaborate fountain decorated with cherubs and reach the famous Globe Inn, which Burns referred to as 'my howff'. The inn dates back to 1610 and includes a Burns Room and the Poet's Chair. It is very atmospheric and you can easily imagine the bard and his cronies spending a merry evening here.

Continue down the High Street. Cross the road, turn left and first right into Burns Street. Follow the road round the parking area and climb the brae to reach Burns House, his home from May 1793 until his death. It contains much interesting memorabilia. Burns' widow Jean Armour continued to live here until she died in 1834.

Cross the major junction at the lights (noting the statue of Jean Armour) and go up steps into St Michael's Kirkyard. This is a fascinating place, crammed with old memorials and gravestones. Many have

Burns associations and are marked as such. Go round to the right of the church to find an information panel. Turn right here and then left to reach the Burns Mausoleum. The poet's body was moved here in 1815, to be joined 20 years later by his widow. Not far away is a Martyrs' Monument to men killed for their Covenanting beliefs.

Burns House, where the poet and his family lived .

From the mausoleum, continue down the path to the end wall and turn left. At the far corner is the site of Burns' original grave. Return past the church, noting the old stones. One unusually commemorates a 'whitesmith', who worked in tin and copper rather than the iron of the blacksmith.

If the church is open you can see a plaque showing where the Burns family had their pew. There is much more of interest in the church, which is said to be on the site of a very ancient chapel founded by St Ninian. The present church dates from 1746 and has fine stained glass, a 1758 working clock and an 1890 Willis organ.

Turn left out of the gates, cross the road and turn left on St Michael's Street, said to be on the line of a Roman road. Turn right down Swan Vennel through the nicely laid-out sheltered housing and follow the path down steps into Dock Park. Turn right along the river. Cross the road at St Michael's Bridge and then cross the fine suspension bridge over the Nith. On the far side, turn right along Kenmure Terrace. No 1 was once the home of the actor John Laurie (Private Fraser in *Dad's Army*).

Enjoy the riverbank walk to the Robert Burns Centre. After visiting the Centre, you can extend the walk a little by following the signs uphill to the Dumfries Museum and Camera Obscura. The latter gives a unique panorama of the town and surrounding countryside.

Devorgilla Bridge.

Return to the riverside, turn left, and pass the Devorgilla Bridge, which has spanned the river here since 1431. At its foot is Old Bridge House, the oldest domestic building in Dumfries (1660) and now a very interesting small museum which includes some rather grisly Victorian dentists' tools.

Continue along the river. Cross the road at the New Bridge and go down steps to the riverside path again (take the lower path, right by the water). Follow this path as far as you can, then come back up and join College Street. After an electricity sub-station, turn right on a path which leads to a new footbridge across the river.

At the far side of the bridge, turn left and follow the riverside path by the Nith, a very pleasant walk. Pass under another bridge, then, just past the end of the wall, go up to the right. Cross the road and go back up Lovers' Walk. The Station Hotel dates from 1897, and the station itself has an original 1858 building on the southbound side.

SANQUHAR

Distance	4km (2.5 miles) circular.
Start and Finish	Sanquhar Station.
Underfoot	Pavement and mostly good paths. Short grassy sections.
Public transport	Regular train service from Glasgow.
Refreshments	Hotels, bars and an excellent tearoom in Sanquhar.
Toilets	South Lochan, near the Tolbooth.
Opening hours	Sanquhar Tolbooth Museum: Apr-Sep Tues-Sat 10.00-13.00 and 14.00-17.00, Sun 14.00-17.00, admission free. Closed on Mondays.

Sanquhar has been a Royal Burgh for over 400 years and its long history is reflected in this walk.

From the station, walk down Station Road past the green with its cairn, unveiled by the Princess Royal, marking the quatercentenary of the Royal Charter in 1998. Turn left, down to the Tolbooth. Designed by William Adam and paid for by the 3rd Duke of Queensberry, it was completed in 1735 and features a handsome double forestair and a flat ogee tower. It holds an excellent local history museum and outside is a seat inscribed 'Never injure a friend'; ironically close to the jougs formerly used to shackle petty criminals!

To the right you can see Burns Lodge, formerly Crichton Hall, birthplace of Dr James Crichton who founded schools in Sanquhar and Dumfries. Also in this area is an intriguing geological pillar made of different types of stone.

Walk down the High Street. The Royal Bank is on the site of a building where Mary Queen of Scots stayed with Lord Crichton after fleeing from the Battle of Langside in May 1568 (see also Walk 8 – Queen's Park). She spent only one further night in Scotland. She is said to have entered the town down the lane now called St Mary's Street.

On the left is Sanquhar Post Office, said to be the oldest in Britain, dating from 1712 and still in use. On the right, a plaque marks the site of the Queensberry Arms or Whigham's Inn, a favourite haunt of Robert Burns, who often stayed here when travelling between Ellisland and Mauchline. He was made a Freeman of the Burgh in 1794.

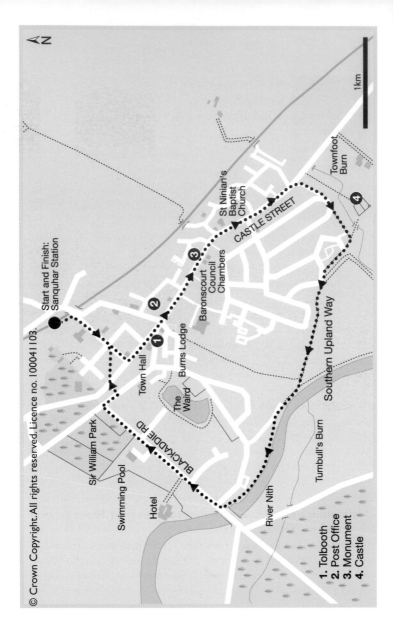

N

Start and Finish: Sanquhar Station

Town Hall

Sir William Park

Swimming Pool

Hotel

BLACKADDIE RD

The Waird

Burns Lodge

Baronscourt Council Chambers

St Ninian's Baptist Church

CASTLE STREET

River Nith

Turnbull's Burn

Southern Upland Way

Townfoot Burn

1km

1. Tolbooth
2. Post Office
3. Monument
4. Castle

On the same side, a little further down, is Baronscourt or Calton Close. Jacobite soldiers lodged here in 1745 and a French prisoner of war from the Napoleonic Wars, Lt Arnaud, was killed near here in a duel. He is buried in Sanquhar Kirkyard.

Across the road is Gallows Close, which formerly led from the old town jail up to the gibbet on the moors above the town. A well here gave prisoners a final drink before they met their fate.

Nearby is a tall granite monument, commemorating the two major 'Sanquhar Declarations'. In 1680, Richard Cameron affixed his Declaration to the Market Cross on this site in direct opposition to Charles II's policy of eliminating Presbyterianism. Cameron, who gave his name to a

Sanquhar Post Office.

famous Scottish regiment, was killed by dragoons near Muirkirk. In 1685, James Renwick fixed a similar Declaration to the Cross. He was eventually hanged in Edinburgh. Opposite the obelisk are the Town Council Chambers, gifted by Lord Glendyne in 1814.

Next left is Leven Street, long known as the Coo Wynd. All townspeople had the right to graze animals on the Muir, and cattle were driven this way for generations. On a gate beside St Ninian's Baptist Church (1841) is a fragment of the old Market Cross of 1680.

Continue down Castle Street. Some of these houses were formerly weavers' cottages. Sanquhar has a long tradition of weaving and also hand knitting with a distinctive pattern of squares and diamonds, most often used in scarves and gloves.

At the end of the houses, turn right on the path and walk towards Sanquhar Castle. Building started in the 12th century, and it is said that William Wallace was here several times – part was called Wallace's Tower. Later visitors included Kings Edward I and II and Mary, Queen

Sanquhar Castle.

of Scots. The castle belonged to the Dukes of Queensberry until it fell into disuse in the 17th century and they moved to the much grander Drumlanrig Castle.

Where the road bends back right, go through the gate and continue on the path behind the houses. Turn briefly right on an access road, then left again with the path, with a playpark to the right. You may notice Southern Upland Way signs. The cross-Scotland path passes through Sanquhar on its 340km journey from Portpatrick, near Stranraer, to Cockburnspath on the Berwickshire coast.

Walk across a field and go through the gate in the stone wall on to a grassy path. There is a fine view across the River Nith to the hills beyond. Set into the wall is a stone carved with the word 'Nith' and also some of the river's tributaries, and just beyond the gate is another carved stone with exotic place names, including Valparaiso, in far distant Chile! There is a good view from here back to the castle.

At a factory, go left down steps and continue on the riverside path, also grassy and with beautiful wild flowers in spring and summer. At a fork, keep left to reach an SUW shelter and information board at a small car park with picnic tables just below Blackaddie Bridge over the Nith.

Turn right along the road past the swimming pool. At the main road (tearoom here) turn right. In 100 metres go left up steps and then cross the green diagonally on a path to return to the station, which still has its original 1850 building in use.

STRANRAER

Distance	4km (2.5 miles) circular.
Start and Finish	Stranraer Railway Station.
Underfoot	Pavement and good paths.
Public transport	Regular train service from Glasgow Central.
Refreshments	Cafes and pubs in the town centre.
Toilets	At the station, Hanover Square car park and Agnew Park.
Opening hours	Stranraer Museum: All year, Mon-Fri 10.00-17.00, Sat 10.00-13.00, 14.00-17.00, free. Castle of St John: April-Sept, Mon-Sat 10.00-13.00, 14.00-17.00, free.

As well as retaining that air of bustle and anticipation which you always find in a port, Stranraer has an interesting town centre with a long history to relate.

From the station, walk towards the town, following the signs. You emerge opposite the North West Castle Hotel, originally built as a residence for Sir John Ross (1777-1856), a noted Arctic explorer.

Cross the road and turn left to reach the beautiful Garden of Friendship, refurbished with help from the TV *Beechgrove Garden* team as a community project and known locally as the Rock Garden. Walk through the garden and rejoin the road. Cross the railway and continue beside the sea with lovely views of Loch Ryan.

Turn right on Ladies Walk. Cross London Road into Westwood Avenue. Swing left with the road and then look for a path on the right, through a small gate and between hedges, that leads over the Black Stank burn and into mature woodland. Follow the path uphill and across the railway. Continue with the path, a very pleasant and shady walk, until you reach the bypass road.

Turn right. There are good views over the town and you can see the main stand at Stair Park, the ground of Stranraer FC. In about 200 metres take the first turning on the right, a small track that winds past a cottage and an electricity substation. Cross an access road and continue on the track. Keep right at a junction.

At the top of the rise you cross the former route of the Stranraer to Portpatrick railway, a branch line long since closed. Portpatrick, about

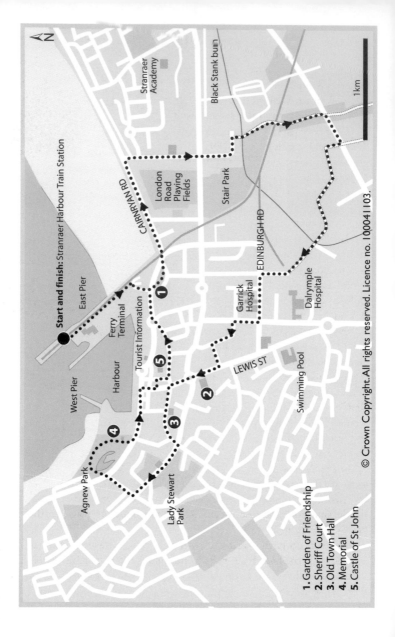

Start and finish: Stranraer Harbour Train Station

East Pier

Ferry Terminal

West Pier

Harbour

Tourist Information

CAIRNRYAN RD

Stranraer Academy

London Road Playing Fields

Black Stank burn

Stair Park

EDINBURGH RD

Garrick Hospital

Dalrymple Hospital

LEWIS ST

Swimming Pool

Agnew Park

Lady Stewart Park

1km

N

© Crown Copyright. All rights reserved. Licence no. 100041103.

1. Garden of Friendship
2. Sheriff Court
3. Old Town Hall
4. Memorial
5. Castle of St John

10km away, is the western terminus of the Southern Upland Way long-distance path, which we met before in Sanquhar (Walk 28).

Walk down Victoria Place and turn left on Edinburgh Road. Pass the Garrick Hospital, noting the fine original building with 1897 datestones. Turn right on Dalrymple Street. Dalrymple and Stair (already met) are family names of the Kennedys, for centuries the largest landowners in this area.

Turn left at Dalrymple Court into Hanover Square. The car park area was once a mass of crowded houses used by Irish immigrants and was known locally as 'Little Ireland'.

Swing right (round the car park) and turn left into Millhill

The Garden of Friendship.

Street, then right into Lewis Street. On the left is the imposing Sheriff Court, built in 1872 as the New Town Hall. Just before Sun Street, note the iron water-pump, given to the town in 1875 by local blacksmith John McWilliam, who had a private well on his property.

Continue down Church Street, passing the parish church of 1841, and turn left into George Street. On the corner is the elegant Old Town Hall of 1776, now housing a good local history museum. Look up to see its fine golden cockerel weathervane. Across the road, the Golden Cross has a door lintel dated 1805 and a 1732 sundial, and the George Hotel's impressive frontage (on the left) is decorated with thistle, shamrock and rose as befits a town much used by travellers (but not the Welsh, apparently).

Bear left up High Street and turn right onto Leswalt High Road. On the left is the Lady Stewart Park and right is the High Kirk of 1843. Its graveyard has superb views across Loch Ryan – an ideal resting place for seamen?

WALK 29

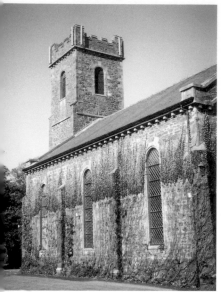

The High Kirk.

Turn right down Park Lane and cross the road into Agnew Park, which has a boating lake and miniature railway. The park may look modest, but can boast the distinction of having being reopened, after refurbishment, by the Queen in 1996. Walk round the pond, which has a fine central fountain and also a couple of islands, and then go right to find the poignant memorial to the 133 people (23 of them from Stranraer) who lost their lives when the ferry *Princess Victoria* sank in January 1953 in a severe gale.

Leave the park and walk along by the harbour. The area to the left is mostly reclaimed land, originally called the Breastwork from the retaining sea wall. The old pier dates from 1820, but modern ferries heading for Belfast and Larne use a newer facility. Note on the left the Art Deco clock tower, dedicated to a local philanthropist, John Simpson.

Turn right into Princes Street, back to George Street, and turn left to reach the Castle of St John, a powerful early 16th-century tower which has amazingly survived intact in the town centre. It was built for the Adair family and was later used as a gaol. In summer you can climb to the top for a superb view of the town and loch.

Outside it are a fountain erected in 1897 to mark Queen Victoria's Diamond Jubilee (moved here from outside the museum) and also a modern stone artwork by Sibylle von Haden called *Tidemarks* and intended to symbolise 4,000 years of the area's history.

Walk down North Strand Street, turn right past the Tourist Information Centre (itself a good 19th-century building), and continue through Port Rodie to return to the station on Railway Pier, opened in 1862.

WALK 29

INDEX

See under general headings for Bridges, Churches, Kings, Parks and Rivers